HOOKED ON BOOKS!

PRENTICE HALL
Englewood Cliffs, New Jersey 07632

HOOKED ON BOOKS!

Activities and Projects That Make Kids Love to Read

PATRICIA TYLER MUNCY

PRENTICE HALL
Englewood Cliffs, New Jersey 07632

10 9 8 7 6 5 4 3 2

Library of Congress Cataloging-in-Publication Data

Muncy, Patricia Tyler.
    Hooked on books! : activities and projects that make kids love to read / Patricia Tyler
Muncy : illustrations by Rebecca Feldman Foster.
        p. cm.
    ISBN 0-87628-411-X
    1. Reading (Elementary) 2. Children—Books and reading. 3. Education, Elementary—
Activity programs. I. Title.
LB1573.M85 1995
372.4—dc20   94-31460
                                                                CIP

Illustrations by Rebecca Feldman Foster

ISBN 0-87628-411-X

THE CENTER FOR APPLIED
RESEARCH IN EDUCATION
CAREER & PERSONAL DEVELOPMENT
A division of Simon & Schuster
West Nyack, New York 10995

Printed in the United States of America

ABOUT THE AUTHOR

Patricia Tyler Muncy was the Reading Supervisor for grades K-12 and the Elementary Supervisor for grades K-4 for Wayne County, Ohio's seven school districts for sixteen years. She retired from that position in the spring of 1993. She is currently an Elementary Consultant for the Holmes County Office of Education in Holmes County, Ohio. She is also an Adjunct Professor for Ashland University. In addition, she is a skilled and popular inservice presenter. She holds a Master's Degree in Reading Supervision and has had a number of years' experience as a classroom teacher and a remedial reading teacher at the elementary school level.

Mrs. Muncy is the author of a variety of practical teaching/learning materials. These include *Word Puzzles* (Fearon Publishers, 1974); *Froggie Alphabet Game* (Ideal School Supply Company, 1976); and seven books of duplicator masters published by Instructor Curriculum Materials—*Word Play, Books A and B* (1977), *Handwriting, Books A, B, and C* (1979), and *Dictionary Skills, Grades 1 and 2* and *Grades 5 and 6* (1980).

She is the author of *Complete Book of Illustrated K-3 Alphabet Games and Activities* (The Center for Applied Research in Education, 1980), *Springboards to Creative Thinking* (The Center for Applied Research in Education, 1985), *The Reading Teacher's Almanac* (The Center for Applied Research in Education, 1991), and is one of the authors of the Scott, Foresman and Company spelling programs *Spelling: Words and Skills* (1984) and *Scott, Foresman Spelling* (1988).

Mrs. Muncy was also on the Editorial Advisory Board of The Center for Applied Research in Education's *Primary Teacher's Ready-to-Use Activities Program*, as well as being a contributing author to that program.

ABOUT THIS BOOK

Hooked on Books! Activities & Projects That Make Kids Love to Read is designed to give teachers of grades K-6 a wealth of ideas and activities to help make students want to read. In a school day full of subjects to be taught and skills to be learned, you can often forget the importance of actively promoting the joys of reading. But you *must make* time to get your students hooked on books!

This book offers over 160 activities, techniques, reading corners, contests, crafts, posters, and bulletin boards you can do with your students to help them develop a lifelong love of books and reading. You'll find, for example, how to:

- set up inviting reading areas where your students can cuddle up with a good book
- make a class favorite-book quilt and other crafts items related to books
- design reading bookmarks and placemats
- have a book character costume party
- create book pennants and posters
- plan and conduct a reading bumper-sticker slogan contest
- have a building-wide sustained silent reading program—during which even the principal and other school staff read, too
- name and decorate school hallways for books
- create classroom bulletin boards
- use book report forms and student reading record pages

Getting students hooked on books should involve not only your class, but the entire school as well. *Hooked on Books!* will help you get *everyone* to enjoy good books and reading. You'll also find full-page activity sheets that you can reproduce as many times as needed for students, as well as guidelines for helping parents to get their children hooked on books at home.

The activities and projects in *Hooked on Books!* are effective whether incorporated into a basal reading, a literature-based, or a whole language instructional program. They are designed to celebrate books and reading, and to ignite children's love of books and reading.

Patricia Tyler Muncy

CONTENTS

SECTION 3
GENERAL HOOKED-ON-BOOKS ACTIVITIES • 33

SECTION 4
SEASONAL BOOK-RELATED ACTIVITIES • 61

SECTION 5
CREATIVE BOOK REPORTS • 73

SECTION 9
READING-MOTIVATION BULLETIN BOARDS • 139

SECTION 10
BOOKMARKS AND BADGES • 169

SECTION 11
POSTERS TO PROMOTE READING • 181

SECTION 12
READING CLIP-ART • 199

SECTION 13
STORY-EXTENSION ACTIVITIES • 207

SECTION 14
BOOK REPORT FORMS TO MOTIVATE READING • 223

SECTION 15
INDIVIDUAL STUDENT READING RECORD PAGES TO PROMOTE
READING FOR PLEASURE • 249

SECTION 16
GUIDING PARENTS TO GET KIDS HOOKED ON BOOKS AT HOME • 281

Section 1

MOTIVATING CHILDREN TO READ THROUGHOUT THE YEAR

FOCUSING ON READING

Many of the ideas and activities in this book are short-term, high-motivation activities designed to prolong the pleasure of a good book or to get kids excited about reading lots of books. This section, however, emphasizes more subtle but highly effective methods you should use day in and day out to instill in your students a lasting love of books and reading.

This section involves the creation of a classroom in which the enjoyment of books and reading is the top priority. It involves implementation of techniques that foster reading, reading, reading!

Underlying the development of this kind of classroom environment is the need to reexamine and reprioritize the way we allocate time in our classrooms, so that there is time each day to read aloud to children, to have a sustained silent reading time, to build in other time for students to read extensively for pleasure and/or information, and time for students to talk together about books they are reading.

So, now let's look at some specific on-going things we can do to insure that our students become real readers, motivated readers, and life-time reading enthusiasts.

TIME WELL SPENT: READING ALOUD TO YOUR STUDENTS

Reading aloud to your students each day is a core, critically important, element in reaching your goal of truly motivating children to read. It is also core to effective reading instruction in general.

Reading aloud to students at all grade levels, K-8, awakens students to the magic of books. It leaves them spellbound, wanting more. It helps nurture the desire to read and promotes the development of a lifetime love of books and reading. Reading aloud to students also helps students build vocabulary/word meaning and a wide variety of comprehension skills.

Sometimes we feel guilty taking time out of the busy school day to read aloud to our students. However, considering the definite value of reading aloud to students, it is important that we *make* time each day. So, relax, grab a good book, and enjoy reading it to your students.

TALK UP BOOKS!

It is important to look for ways to talk up books day after day throughout the school year. You will want to find opportunities to mention good books the class has enjoyed.

Sometimes you may want to tell the class about a terrific book you were reading the night before. Once in a while you may want to mention that you have just finished a book that was so good you just couldn't put it down until the end. Tell them how you kept on reading until four o'clock in the morning because you just couldn't stop. Then have the students tell about their similar experiences. You may want to designate a section of chalkboard on which students are to place their signatures if they have kept on reading a book long after they were supposed to be asleep. Another time you may want to have them sign their names on a poster if they ever read by flashlight under the covers at night.

On a rainy afternoon you may want to longingly look at a book that you have been reading during sustained silent reading time and tell your students that on rainy afternoons at home you like to curl up in the armchair in your living room and read all afternoon.

On a snowy day, when the snow is coming down hard and heavy, you might want to mention that this is just the kind of day you like to bury yourself in a good book. You might even set aside the lesson plans for the afternoon and let your students bury themselves in good books, reading just for pleasure.

The possibilities for talking up books and reading are unlimited.

THE "SELL" TECHNIQUE

The "sell" technique is another way of talking up books. It simply involves every few days selecting three or four good books you are certain your students will enjoy reading and with which you are familiar. Then all you do is stand in front of the class, hold up one of the books, enthusiastically tell a little bit about the book, and tell the students why you think they will enjoy reading it. Then place the book on the chalkholder of the chalkboard.

Follow a similar procedure with each of the remaining books. Then watch your students latch on to those books!

THE "BAIT AND LURE" TECHNIQUE

The "bait and lure" technique is sure-fire. It involves selecting a book you are certain students will enjoy reading at your grade level. Read aloud the first chapter or two to your class or to a reading group. Read enough so that the students are really hooked on the book. Then place a bookmark in the book and place it on the chalkholder of the chalkboard. Tell your students that they can check the book out one at a time and continue reading this great story on their own. Your students will eagerly snap up that book and continue reading it on their own.

This technique can be used every couple of weeks.

STUDENTS "SELL" THEIR BOOKS

Give students an opportunity to "sell" their books to their classmates. Whenever a student has read a particularly good book, ask that student to tell the rest of the class about the book and what made it such a good book. Ask that the student tell just enough about the book to make the rest of the class want to read it.

Students who wish to carry it a step further can prepare a poster advertising the book in advance of telling the class about it. This poster can be posted on the bulletin board after they "sell" their book orally to the class.

The students' "selling" of books to their classmates should come from a real desire on the part of the students to share information and enthusiasm about a really great book they think their classmates should know about and would like to read. This should not become a book report assignment activity.

IT PAYS TO DISPLAY

If we want to entice children to read library books in their spare time, we need to display books attractively around the classroom. We also need to rotate those books fairly frequently so that new books are constantly luring children to read.

Books can be displayed on windowsills, chalkholders of chalkboards, tables, display racks—just all over the place. The more books, the better.

Do not worry if your classroom library is somewhat limited. You can easily obtain lots of additional books for display and student reading from your school library and the local public library.

AN INVITING SPOT

Establishing an inviting "reading corner" in your classroom can certainly encourage students to pick up a book and settle down for good reading.

The possibilities for creating a reading corner are many. Here are some ideas.

A donated used piece of carpet, a second-hand sofa, a couple of large throw pillows, and a bookcase loaded with books can form the basis for a comfortable reading spot.

A couple of second-hand recliner chairs, an old rocking chair, and a bookcase filled with wonderful books can become the "in" reading spot in the classroom.

Carpet samples obtained inexpensively from a carpet store can be stacked near a bookcase in your classroom, along with some throw pillows and some prop-up cushions. Students can grab a book, a couple carpet samples, and a pillow or prop-up cushion, then stretch out comfortably to read.

If you want to get really fancy— and if you have a funding source for the construction materials— you might want to consider a reading loft with a partially enclosed carpeted reading area below, and a ladder leading to a carpeted reading loft above. Built-in bookcases on each level filled with marvelous books and a large number of throw pillows complete the reading loft.

NOTE: Sturdy construction and railing for safety are, of course, essential. Laying down rules for safe use of the loft will also be necessary.

An old-fashioned bathtub with claw feet can sometimes be purchased at an auction or retrieved from someone's remodeling throwaway pile. Place the scrubbed bathtub in a carpeted corner of your classroom. Now, in your best begging voice, ask a local carpet store if it will donate a carpet remnant and an installer to line the inside of the bathtub with the carpet.

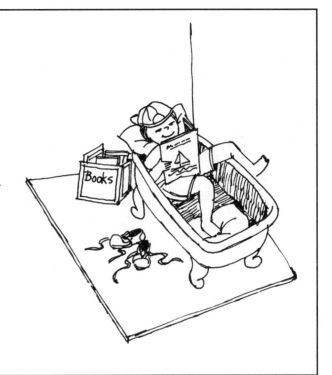

Add some soft throw pillows to the carpet-lined bathtub and you will have a marvelous reading spot your students will scramble to use. When the tub is occupied, other students can sit or sprawl on the carpeted area around the tub and read.

If your school is in a farming community or if you just want something different, you might like this one. First, place a piece of used carpet or a carpet remnant in the area in which you want to have your reading corner. Next, place 2 or 3 old, but clean tractor tires here and there on the carpet. (Used tractor tires can be purchased inexpensively from tire stores in rural areas.) Next, add a number of throw pillows to the area, some inside the tractor tires, some outside. Now, add some piles of thoroughly delightful books and you have a reading spot. Your students will enjoy sitting inside, sitting on, sprawling across, and propping themselves against the tractor tires as they read for pleasure.

Students in the primary grades will enjoy a teddy bear reading corner. Begin by putting down a used piece of carpet or a carpet remnant. Add some pillows and perhaps a comfortable chair or two. Then add a number of teddy bears here and there. Students can come to the reading corner, latch on to a teddy bear, and settle down comfortably to read while cuddling a teddy bear or to read softly to the teddy bear.

Of course, any classroom reading corner can be further decorated to fit with a special theme or unit. For example, the reading corner can be decorated to look like a jungle one month and an ocean floor another month to fit with units being studied.

SUSTAINED SILENT READING

Providing daily *sustained silent reading* (SSR) time is an absolute must in the school-day lesson plan if you want to nurture a life-long love of books and reading in your students. If your school has implemented daily sustained silent reading time building-wide, you are all set. If your school does not have sustained silent reading time, it is up to you to establish it on a permanent daily basis in your classroom.

To institute SSR in your classroom, you will want to set a 15- to 20-minute time period each day during which students (and teacher) put aside everything and simply read for their own pleasure from books and magazines of their choice.

The teacher reading for pleasure in a book of his or her choice during SSR time is important, too. Many students never see an adult at home read a book or magazine. We tell students about the importance of reading and the pleasure of reading. But, if in their "real" world they never see adults reading, there is a believability gap. We want to let kids see us reading and enjoying books during SSR time!

One of the great things about SSR time is that during that 15 to 20 minutes of reading a library book, most students will get far enough into the book that they will be eager to continue reading the first chance they get. That means, for many of your students, they will grab that book and continue reading whenever they get an opportunity—when they get through with an assignment early and any other spare minutes during the school day. It also increases the likelihood of students willingly and eagerly taking library books home to continue reading. What more could we want?

GOING BEYOND THE BASAL

Too often students think reading is boring or just plain hard work. They think of reading as just reading in the basal reading book and doing lots and lots of workbook pages and worksheets. This type of reading instruction produces a lot of good readers as well as a number of poor readers. This type of instruction also produces a large number of students who simply do not enjoy reading, who do not choose to read for pleasure, and who never discover the enchantment of books!

If you are using a basal textbook, workbook pages, and worksheets as the main component of your reading program, you may want to begin purchasing some sets of paperback books to use in addition to your basal reading books. Taking a reading group out of the basal and into a good paperback book periodically can rekindle students' interest in reading. Students can read in the paperback book independently, then come to the reading group for a lively discussion of the plot, characters, etc.

As you begin taking your students out of the basal and into a good paperback book, you will find the students' reactions so positive that you will probably find yourself requesting more sets of paperback books. Over a period of time, you will probably find yourself relying less on the basal reading book and incorporating more "real" children's literature into your reading instructional program. Eventually, you will find yourself developing meaningful skill lessons in the context of good children's books as well as excellent reading extension activities that really involve students and increase their level of learning.

Try it. You'll love it and so will your students!

WARNING: SKILL/DRILL OVERDOSE KILLS

Too many skill/drill pages kill students' enjoyment of reading and waste a lot of valuable reading time.

In many classrooms students are assigned many skill/drill workbook pages and worksheets each day to fill up reading seatwork time. Typically these workbook pages and worksheets are primarily of an isolated skill/drill type.

The quality and quantity of learning gained from the time spent on these worksheets can be limited. For higher reading-ability students, the worksheets are very easy and usually not needed. These students already know those skills and could use that seatwork skill/drill time more productively by reading.

Average reading-ability students find themselves working about two-thirds of the total allocated reading instruction time each day on skill/drill materials that often seem repetitive or for which they do not see the importance. Many of these students become turned off to reading in general because of the large amount of skill/drill assignments.

The lower reading-ability students are even more turned off on reading by the skill/drill pages. They usually have a considerable degree of difficulty doing the worksheets and workbook pages. They often do them with a high level of error and frustration. In addition, much of this isolated skill practice does not carry over to application in real reading situations.

While students do need to learn phonics and word attack skills and do need to develop an array of comprehension skills, the heavy use of independent worksheets and workbook pages to teach or drill these skills needs to be critically reevaluated. We know that, like any skill, reading skill is best developed by letting students read, read, read! And, we know that the more children discover the enchanting stories in books, the more they will enjoy reading. Likewise, the more they enjoy reading, the more they *will* read.

With this in mind, we need to provide children with *much* more time to read library books for pleasure. To provide this time, we need to cut back greatly on the worksheets and workbook pages and free them to read.

TRADE BOOKS IN THE CONTENT AREAS

Using trade books in the content areas can be a very effective way of bringing social studies alive and adding depth of understanding in science.

You may want to read aloud to your students a good historical fiction that fits in with the period you are studying in social studies. A well-selected book can enhance your students' learning in a way that no social studies book can ever begin to do.

Sometimes you may want to beg, borrow, or purchase several sets of paperback historical fiction and biography books that fit in with the social studies topic. The sets of books can be at different levels of difficulty to accommodate the different reading levels of students in your class. The class can then be divided into groups and each group assigned one or more books to read. The groups can then prepare projects or presentations based on their books.

You may also want to visit the library and gather together a collection of factual books relating to a topic in the science textbook. Then, after the class has read and discussed the lesson in the science textbook, let them really begin learning about the topic(s) in depth. Let them do research individually, in pairs, or in cooperative learning groups, using the books you have collected.

You will find using trade books in your science and social studies classes such a powerful tool in reaching students and actively engaging students that you will begin to wonder how you ever taught any other way!

BOOK DISCUSSION GROUPS

Think back to when you were a child. Do you remember what you wanted to do when you had just finished reading a terrific book? Do you remember just having to tell someone about the book? Do you remember enthusiastically telling mom or dad or a friend about what happened in the story? Do you remember how extra great it was when that other person had also read that book and you could *really* talk about the book together, comparing favorite parts, discussing a character's behavior, speculating about what happened after the book ended?

Most children today react to a terrific book the same way you did. They feel the same bursting desire to tell someone about the story. They want someone else to understand the depth of emotion they felt, the funny situations in the book, how the mystery developed and was solved or just the wonderfulness of the story.

We can and should be fostering students' strong desire to talk about books they are reading or have finished reading. We need to encourage students to get into discussion groups and simply—informally—talk about the book(s) they are reading.

A book discussion group can be made up of as few as two students or as many as five or six students. The students can talk about a book they have all read, sharing their reactions and feelings, discussing the plot, etc. Or, the students in the group can excitedly tell each other about any good book they have just finished reading. Book discussion group time can be built into the schedule or it can just occur spontaneously. Book discussion groups work especially well fourth grade and up, but can many times work successfully at a third-grade level.

The key to an effective book discussion in this context is simply letting the students interact with each other, talking about the book(s). It is not a teacher-led discussion; it is student led.

Usually there is no difficulty letting small groups of students get together to talk about books they are reading or have read. The talk is enthusiastic and spontaneous. If, however, the discussion in some of the book discussion groups is boring, flat or stilted, you may need to model how to talk about a book and how to interact with other students discussing a story.

The easiest way to model the process is to note a student book discussion group that is going well. Ask the students in that group to show the rest of the class how to discuss books. Then have the rest of the students listen while the students in the selected discussion group model the process.

If none of the discussion groups would be a good example for the modeling process, you may need to model how a discussion group works. If that is the case, select a book you know is a favorite of children at your grade. Read or re-read the book so that you have the story fresh in your mind. Next, select three or four students who are enthusiastic book readers and who like to talk about books they are reading to help you show the rest of the class how a book discussion group works.

Have the selected students join you with books they want to talk about. You can sit on the floor or around a table, and ask the rest of the class to watch and listen. Now, begin to sincerely and enthusiastically talk about the book you have read. Encourage others in the group who have read the book to interact, talking about the best parts. Don't monopolize the time. Let the various students in the model group talk and interact on the books they want to talk about. Keep the modeling session brief so that the students who are watching get the idea but don't get bored or fidgety. In reality, this means you will probably have to halt the book discussion group part way through the discussion.

After the students have watched the modeling of interaction in a book discussion group, brainstorm together as a class what makes a book discussion group work well. You may even want to list student ideas on the chalkboard. The modeling of the book discussion process and discussing effective book discussions will result in better quality discussions and interactions.

READING RESPONSE JOURNALS

Reading response journals for grades 4-6 can serve to fan students' interest in books and reading. Reading response journals can, also, very effectively increase students' understanding of plot, character, setting, and various techniques writers use.

To begin the use of reading response journals in your classroom, each student must have a journal to be used only as a reading response journal. The journals might be spiral-bound notebooks provided by the school or by the individual students. Or, they could be "homemade."

To create homemade journals, simply give each student 8 to 10 sheets of white photocopier paper and a piece of wallpaper from a wallpaper sample book.* To make the journal, the students stack the sheets of white paper evenly and then fold them in half. Next, they fold their sheets of wallpaper in half and insert the folded paper into the folded wallpaper "cover." Now, using a stapler, the students staple the pages and the cover together in several spots about 1/3" from the fold seam. Last of all, have the students bring their journal "creations" to you so that you can trim off the excess wallpaper from the three open-edge sides. Violà, very inexpensive reading journals.

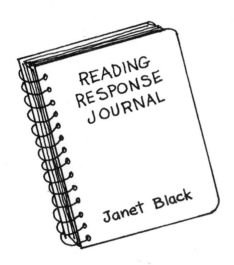

Tell the students that they are to write in their reading journals each time they finish reading a book. They are to address the journal entry to a classmate or to the teacher. The journal entry should tell the person it is addressed to something meaningful about the book they have read. It could discuss the skill with which the author writes; it could discuss specific characteristics of the story that made the book outstanding, average, or below expectation; and it could also point out why the person to whom the journal entry is addressed would or would not enjoy the book. If the student who is writing the journal entry knows that the person to whom the entry is addressed has read the book, the entry could also seek the other student's reactions to specific parts in the story or to techniques used by the author.

The possible content of the journal entry is wide open. The only requirement is that it consist of meaningful reaction of some type to the book. Just saying, "This was a good book. I liked it. I think you will like it, too," is not enough.

After the journal entry is complete, the student should give the journal to the person to whom he or she has addressed that entry. The person who receives the journal reads it, writes a meaningful response on the next page of the journal, and returns the journal to its owner.

---

* Wallpaper sample books can be obtained free or at very little cost from wallpaper stores.

Require that the students address a journal entry to you, the teacher, once a month, every third book read, or whatever frequency you wish to designate. You will certainly want student journals coming to you on a staggered basis so that you will not be snowed under trying to read each reading response journal and respond in their journals in a meaningful, thoughtful manner on a single evening or weekend!

Students will soon become very comfortable writing in their journals and responding meaningfully to each other's entries. As you come across a particularly thoughtful, well-written, or insightful reading response entry, read it aloud to the class and point out some of the reasons why it is good. In this way students will be hearing examples of good entries. Over a period of time the caliber of some of the lesser quality entries will begin to improve.

As students read each other's reading response journal entries, they will be making a mental note of books they want to read. They will also really get in to meaningfully talking about books. In addition, students reading and responding to each other's reading response journals helps students internalize an enthusiasm about books and a critical appreciation of the writer's craft.

VARIATION

Instead of having students write in their reading response journals each time they finish a book, you may want to designate one or two days a week when all students will write in their journals. The entries in the journals would be based on reaction or comments on a book they are in the process of reading or have finished reading. This would increase the frequency of student journal entries and responses to entries.

THE READING EXPECTATION

As teachers, we need to just expect our students to pick up a library book and read whenever they have spare minutes during the school day. From the first day of school in the fall, we need to be conveying the pleasure and knowledge to be found in books. We need to convey that books are so wonderful that it would be great if we could just read them all day. However, even though that is impossible, they can find many opportunities throughout the school day—spare minutes here and there—that they can spend enjoying reading their library books.

That mind-set, plus talking-up books, radiating enthusiasm about the marvelous stories found in books, and encouraging students to search for opportunities to get back to their library books, will have a definite impact on how students spend extra time during the school day.

Your clear and positive expectation of their reading and enjoying books in all spare minutes will result in this happening. Your expectations have a powerful impact on student behavior!

IMMERSE YOURSELF IN CHILDREN'S BOOKS

To maximize student enthusiasm about books, you must be able to meaningfully discuss specific books with students, recommend books to individual students and groups of students, select books to read aloud to the class, choose appropriate books for instructional purposes, and, in general, enthusiastically talk up books and authors. In order to do this, you *must* be very familiar with a large number of children's books.

Your school librarian or a children's librarian at your local public library will be delighted to make recommendations of outstanding books appropriate for your grade level. Walk out of the library with an armful of books. When you get home, find a comfortable chair and begin enjoying the wonderful world of children's literature! Once you start reading children's books, you'll find it hard to stop!

Even if you have the busiest of schedules, make a resolution to read a minimum of a specific number of children's books per month—then keep that resolution.

As you become familiar with more and more children's books, you will find yourself frequently using that knowledge to select books for use in your classroom and to really talk books with children.

Section 2

ACTIVITIES TO PROLONG THE PLEASURE OF A GOOD BOOK

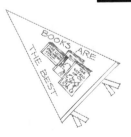

BOOK CHARACTER PLATES

Let your students make a truly permanent memory of a favorite book. Have them create book character plates with drawings of favorite book characters permanently molded into dishwasher-safe, 10" melamine plates.

First, you will need to order a Small Fry Plate Kit from:

> Small Fry Originals
> P.O. Box 769045
> Dallas, Texas 75376-9045
> Phone: 214-330-8671

Each kit costs approximately $3.95 and comes with 50 die-cut drawing sheets, a set of markers, and instructions. When you send the completed artwork to Small Fry Originals to be molded into plastic plates, there is an additional charge of approximately $2.75 per plate, plus postage and handling. (NOTE: Verify all prices with the company before sending any money.)

Once your plate kit has arrived, you will be ready to implement this memorable book-extension activity with your students. Have each student select a favorite book character that he or she wants to depict on a plastic plate. The students can draw the character free-handed onto the die-cut drawing sheet, or can find a picture of the character in a book and trace it onto the drawing sheet. (The drawing sheet is thin enough that when it is placed over an illustration, the illustration will show through. Students will be able to trace the illustration easily.)

Colored markers are provided in the kit. First-, second- and third-graders should use only those markers in drawing (or tracing) and coloring their book characters.

With older students (fourth grade and up) you may want to get a little more daring to achieve *very* beautiful results. The directions that come with the kit indicate that only the markers that come with the kit will work when the company molds the artwork into a plate. However, *good* quality colored pencils (Venus® Colored Pencils and Prismacolor® colored pencils) and fine-line Flair® Pens seem to work just as well. Allowing the students to use your good colored pencil set and fine-line Flair® Pens to create their drawing can result in plates with artwork that is truly outstanding!

If you do decide to allow your students to use your sets of good colored pencils and fine-line Flair® Pens to create their book character illustrations, the company will not guarantee the results. However, after experimenting with using colored pencils and Flair® Pens, the key to the artwork being molded into flawless plates seems to rest more with the students keeping the artwork clean, grease free, and wrinkle free. This means that students should carefully wash and dry their hands before working on the artwork for their plates. It also means that they should use utmost care in handling the artwork to avoid wrinkles, creases, and smudges. If this care is not taken, the artwork will not properly mold into the plate and bubbles will appear in the plastic surface of the plate whether the kit markers are used or whether a combination of kit markers, good quality colored pencils, and Flair® Pens are used!

It is up to you to decide whether to let your students use only the markers that come with the kit or to assume a slight additional risk that some of the plates might not seal properly in the molding process by letting students also use good colored pencils and Flair® fine-line pens. Regardless, this is an exciting way to let students permanently prolong the enjoyment of a good book. Without a doubt, this is a book-promoting activity your students will remember with pleasure for years to come! In addition, parents will truly treasure the book character plates created by their children!

SHRINK-PLASTIC BOOK CHARACTER NECKLACES AND KEY CHAINS

This unique activity allows students to prolong the pleasure of a good book by making delightful book character necklaces or key chains out of shrink plastic.

You'll need shrink plastic*, permanent black fine-line Sharpie® Pens, colored pencils (Venus® or Paradise® Colored Pencil Sets work best), scissors, hole punch, yarn (for necklaces), key chains (for key chain projects), non-stick cookie sheet or aluminum foil and a standard cookie sheet, and toaster oven or regular oven.

*Shrink plastic comes in 8 1/2" × 10" sheets. Pictures are drawn on the plastic. When the plastic is baked in a 300° oven for 30 seconds to 2 minutes, the plastic shrinks to approximately one-third size. At the same time, the plastic thickens and the colors of the drawing intensify. The resulting finished product is a delightful miniaturized version of the original.

Sheets of shrink plastic can be purchased from many craft stores. Or it can be ordered under the name of "Shrinky Dinks" from:

K & B Innovations, Inc.
P.O. Box 66
Brookfield, WI 53005
Phone: 414-966-7550

If ordering shrink plastic from K & B Innovations, call to check current price. A 20-sheet pack will cost approximately $6.00. A 200-sheet pack will cost approximately $50.00. Key chains can also be ordered from K & B Innovations.

If you are buying shrink plastic from a craft store, be sure to purchase sheets that have a matt finish on one side. The matt finish allows the students to use colored pencils to color their book character pictures.

PROCEDURE

Cut a sheet of 8 1/2" × 10" shrink plastic into halves or quarters, keeping in mind that the plastic will shrink to about one third that size when baked. Give each student a piece of shrink plastic. Have each student select a favorite book character from a book you read aloud to the students or from books they have read individually or as a group. Have the students draw or trace their book character pictures onto the matt-finished side of the plastic, remembering to draw the pictures larger than the desired finished size. Permanent fine-line markers and colored pencils will work well in drawing and coloring the book characters on the shrink plastic. (Do not use nonpermanent ink marking pens or crayons.) Be aware that uncolored areas will shrink frosted. Therefore, when white is desired, the student should color the area with a white colored pencil.

You may wish to provide outline pictures of various book characters for younger children to trace onto the plastic. Or, students can find an illustration of the character in the book, place the shrink plastic on top of it, and trace.

When the students are finished drawing/tracing and coloring the book character illustration on their shrink plastic, use scissors to round corners of the shrink plastic. Then, punch a hole in the plastic with a regular hand-held hole punch.

Now the items are ready for shrinking. The shrinking can be done in a toaster oven or regular oven. (NOTE: A microwave oven will *NOT* shrink the shrink plastic.) Preheat the oven to 300°. Place the shrink plastic piece(s) on a non-stick cookie sheet or a regular cookie sheet that is covered with aluminum foil. Place in the oven for approximately two minutes. The shrink plastic pieces will lie almost flat when they have finished shrinking. To flatten any shrink plastic pieces that do not come out totally flat, remove them from the oven and cookie sheet and place on a flat surface. Then put some weight on them to hold the pieces flat as they cool.

It works best to only shrink two or three pieces at a time just in case you should need to flatten them further. If you try to shrink too many at a time, some of the pieces that might need further flattening may be too cool by the time you get to them.

When the shrink plastic has cooled, students can thread yarn through the hole to make necklaces or put a key chain through the hole to make a key chain.

The resulting book character necklaces and key chains are truly terrific and will be treasured by the students. This is indeed a memorable activity to honor a memorable book!

FAVORITE BOOK T-SHIRT

Here is another great way to let grade 4 and up students extend the pleasure of a favorite book. Tell your students they are going to make favorite book T-shirts. Ask each student to bring a white or light colored T-shirt to class. Tell the students that if the T-shirt is brand new, it should be washed before bringing it to school.

In the meantime, you will need to get several boxes of Stanford's® Glad Rags Fabric and Leather Decorating Markers (purchase from a school supply catalog or from a local fabric or craft store) and/or assorted colors of fabric paints (available at local fabric shops, craft stores, discount stores, etc.). You will also need a stack of old newspapers.

To begin the activity, have each student think of a favorite book to portray on his or her T-shirt. The students may wish to find copies of the books they have selected to help them in drawing a picture representing that book on their T-shirts. Give each student several sheets of newspaper to insert inside the T-shirt to keep the fabric markers or fabric paints from penetrating through the surface on which they are working and onto the side of the shirt underneath the work area.

Now, students create an illustration of a book character or scene from his or her favorite book on his or her shirt using the fabric markers or fabric paints. Students may also choose to print the title of the book on the T-shirt.

Your students will be proud of their T-shirts and will be eager to wear them to school! Have a "Book T-Shirt Day" the day following the completion of the T-shirts when all of the students will proudly wear their T-shirts to school.

FAVORITE BOOK QUILT

This activity is really special! It involves some expense for materials and needs someone with a knowledge and willingness to volunteer to put together and sew a patchwork quilt. However, the results are truly fabulous and worth the expense and effort. In fact, the results are worthy of permanent display on a wall in the main hall or the school library.

For this activity, your students will be creating a Favorite Book Quilt. Using fabric markers and/or fabric paints, the students will draw pictures of their favorite book characters on fabric squares. The fabric squares will then be patched together, then quilted into a quilt by some wonderful parent volunteer who knows how to quilt (or, by you, the teacher, if you know how to quilt).

To get this started, you will need the guidance of someone who knows how to quilt. Purchase white fabric, the cotton batting that is used inside the quilt, and fabric of a contrasting rich, solid color to form the underside and border of the quilt. Navy, royal blue, burgundy, or green are good color possibilities to consider. You will also need spools and spools of white thread.

The next step is to explain the project to the students. If your students are unfamiliar with quilts, you may need to show them an actual quilt or a picture of one so that they understand what you are talking about. You will also need to talk about how quilts are made. You may wish to have the individual who will actually be quilting the quilt explain the process to the students.

Next, have each student think of a special book character he or she would like to honor with a patch on a quilt. When each student has selected a character, give the students a square piece of paper the size of the piece of fabric on which they will be working. On this paper, they can sketch a preliminary drawing of the character they have chosen. Be sure they leave room to print the name of the book character and/or the title of the book. Be sure they also leave a half-inch border on all four sides to allow for the stitching together of the patches.

Once they have finished their preliminary drawings, they are ready to begin drawing their pictures on the fabric. Give each student a square of the white fabric and let them begin drawing and coloring with fabric markers and fabric paints.

When the students have finished their artwork on the patches, it is time for your quilting volunteer to take the pieces home and begin putting the quilt together and quilting it. The quilting process will probably take a couple of months. But, the end product will be well worth the wait!

When the quilt is finished, your students will be delighted and very proud of themselves. You may want to contact the local newspaper to take a picture and write an article for publication. You may want to exhibit it at the next PTA meeting for well-deserved admiration. You may also want to make arrangements to have it displayed at the local public library or the storefront window of a local department store. Ultimately, you will probably want to find a special display location in your school. Or, perhaps you will want to use it as a wonderful, one-of-a-kind wall hanging in your own home.

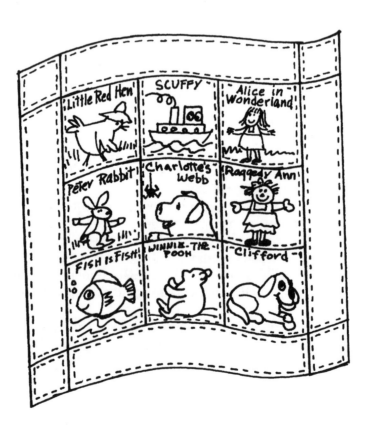

FAVORITE BOOK ELECTIONS

Lead the class in talking about some of the books they have enjoyed reading. After a number of books have been mentioned, begin listing some of the best-liked ones on the chalkboard. After twelve or more books have been listed on the chalkboard, ask the students to narrow the list down to their favorite five books. This is done through discussion and interaction among the students. Circle on the chalkboard the names of the five books the students selected.

Then, write the title of each book on separate sheets of paper. Place each sheet of paper in a different location in the classroom. Ask the students to each decide which of those books is his or her favorite and move to that location.

The class is now divided into favorite book teams. Each team's task now is to plan, create, and implement a campaign—including the use of posters, slogans and speeches—to persuade another class to select the book as its favorite in favorite book elections.

Let the students actually create, develop, and execute their campaigns for their selected books. Their target "voters" should be another class at their grade level. If the school has only one class at each grade level, the target "voters" should be the class one grade level above theirs.

Excitement and persuasive techniques increase in intensity as the campaigns proceed. On a designated day, the target class votes on "official ballots." A team of official non-partisan judges count the votes, as the two participating classes watch. With the announcement of the winning book, the winning team can make victory speeches and celebrate the victory with their "voters."

What a way to let the fun of books shine through!

BOOK MOBILES

Your students will enjoy creating book mobiles. Let each child make a mobile representing a good book he or she has recently finished reading. The mobiles can be made of colored posterboard and yarn. Drawings of characters and/or scenes from the book can be suspended from a strip of cardboard on which the title of the book has been printed.

The finished mobiles can be hung from the classroom, hallway, or school library ceiling.

Creating mobiles can serve as a means of letting the students prolong their pleasure of a good book or can be an excellent alternative to the traditional book report.

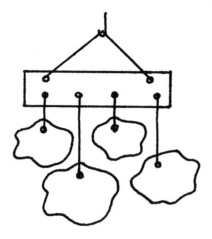

CLAY-DOUGH BOOK CHARACTERS

Your students will enjoy making clay-dough book characters to represent favorite book characters.

You'll need:

8 cups flour
2 cups salt
3 cups water
mixing bowl
several small bowls of water
several garlic presses
toothpicks
3-4 nails
waxed paper
paper clips
cookie sheets
tempera paints and/or acrylic paints
shellac
an oven

PREPARATION

Prepare clay dough by mixing together 8 cups of flour, 2 cups of salt, and 3 cups of water to form a stiff dough.

PROCEDURE

Give each student a chunk of clay dough and a piece of waxed paper on which to model their clay dough. Let students model their book characters, forming shapes approximately 1/2″ to 1″ thick. The book character possibilities are end-less—from people to lions, puppies, teddy bears, lambs, and elves.

Clay-dough features can be added or molded into the character shapes. Clay dough can be pressed through a garlic press to form hair. This "hair" can be attached to the character by moistening the surface with water and pressing it into place. Eyes and other features can be indented into the surface using a tooth-pick or a nail. Eyes and other features can also be made by rolling small balls of clay dough and attaching them by moistening the surfaces and pressing into place.

Embedding a paper clip in the dough before baking makes it easy to hang the clay-dough characters for easy display or for use as Christmas tree orna-ments.

Next, you will need to place the completed clay-dough characters on a bak-ing sheet, placed well apart so that they won't touch as they spread in the baking process. Bake the clay-dough sculptures in a 325° oven for approximately 15-20 minutes. Be careful not to over cook, as this will result in cracking or burning.

The clay-dough characters will puff somewhat as they bake. Parts that are attached together will bond together in the baking process.

When the clay-dough book characters have cooled, they can be painted with tempera paints or acrylic paints. When the paint is dry, they can be covered with shellac.

Your students will be delighted with their clay-dough characters. All you will need to do is decide on a creative and effective way to display their book charac-ters. Put on your creative thinking cap and think up something terrific!

BOOK CHARACTER DOLL DAY

Have each child in the class dress a doll or a stuffed animal to represent a book character. Then have the children bring their dolls or stuffed animals for a Book Character Doll Day. The dolls and stuffed animals can be displayed with identifi-cation cards placed in front of each one indicating the character being portrayed.

A committee of teachers can serve as judges in selecting winning book char-acter dolls. Or, they can simply be displayed without judging.

CRAYON ETCHINGS

Your students will enjoy making crayon etchings of scenes from books. Give each student a sheet of heavy white art paper. Have the students crayon heavily over the entire front of the paper. They may use one color or a variety of colors, but the page should be solidly colored. Next, have the students dust their papers with tal-cum powder, then brush India ink evenly over the entire surface of the paper. Let the papers dry overnight.

Have each student select a favorite scene from a book he or she has read. Using the point of a pair of school scissors, each student can etch a scene from the book onto the specially prepared paper. As the scene is etched onto the paper, the ink is scraped off of the surface and the colors under the ink will show through attractively. When the scene is finished, the title of the book can be etched across the top of the page.

The book scene pictures can be used to form an interesting bulletin board display in the classroom or the school library.

MURALS

Let the class make a mural depicting scenes from a good book you have read aloud to the class. The scenes can be sketched, then painted with tempera paint on a long piece of kraft paper, butcher paper, or shelf paper. Hang the completed mural on the classroom wall as a reminder of a good book enjoyed by all.

BOOK CHARACTER BATH SPONGES

Have each student bring a new, unused sponge to class. Each student then selects a favorite book character that he or she would like to draw on his or her sponge. Now, let the students draw the book characters on their sponges using fabric marking pens or permanent felt-tip markers.

The completed sponges become Book Character Bath Sponges, ready to be taken home by the student and used for bathing.

IN HONOR OF THE BOOK

Have a special day when the students honor a special book loved by the whole class. On this day everyone in the class comes to school dressed as one of the characters in the book. Special games, activities, and assignments can be developed to emphasize the special book of the day.

This is an excellent way to extend the enjoyment of a book read aloud to the class and thoroughly loved by all.

The Wizard of Oz Day

Winnie-the-Pooh Day

Huckleberry Finn Day

FAVORITE BOOK PLACEMATS

Making placemats depicting favorite book characters or scenes can be a way to let students prolong the pleasure of books they read and enjoyed.

Give each student a large sheet of white paper approximately the size of a placemat. Have the students draw pictures of several of their favorite book characters to make book character placemats. Pictures should be drawn with colored pencils or washable markers. Avoid crayons because the wax will melt when the placemats are laminated. The name of the character can be written under each picture.

To make favorite book placemats, each student selects a favorite book and draws pictures of characters and scenes from the book. The title of the book is then written on the placemat.

Finished placemats should be laminated to make them usable and reusable as real placemats. Students may choose to make one placemat or a set of placemats for use at home.

VARIATION

This could be a whole school activity. The (better) placemats can be given to a local restaurant to be used on their tables. Patrons of the restaurant will enjoy the students' placemats!

A LETTER TO THE AUTHOR

Writing a letter to a favorite author can be a worthwhile activity. Let the class vote to determine the favorite author of the majority of the students in the class. Then have the class compose a letter to that author, telling the author how much the class has enjoyed his or her book(s). The letter should mention favorite characters, scenes, etc. One student can be selected to copy the class letter on stationery. The letter can be sent to the author in care of his or her publishing company. The publisher will usually forward the letter to the author, if possible.

Many authors will write a letter back to the class!

VARIATION

Each student can decide on a favorite author to whom he or she would like to write a letter. The key to individual letters by individual students is that each letter should be sincere and should mention *specific* things the reader enjoyed in the book. The letters could also ask well thought-out questions. The key to good individual letters is that they are sincere and well thought out, not just the completion of an assignment.

Section 3

General Hooked-on-Books Activities

"DO NOT DISTURB" DOORKNOB SIGNS

Two of the most powerful ways to ensure that students develop a love of books and reading is to read aloud to your students *every* day and to provide time *daily* for students to read independently in trade books (library books and paperback books).

Beyond providing time daily for these, you can convey to the students in your classroom—and to all of the students and teachers (and principal, too) in your school—the importance you place on reading for pleasure. Photocopy the two "Do Not Disturb" signs onto coverstock (index card-weight 9" × 12" paper that comes in various colors). Laminate the signs. Then cut them out, including the doorknob holes. Now your signs are ready for use.

Put the "Do Not Disturb—Teacher Reading Aloud" sign on the outside doorknob of your classroom door just before you begin to read a story aloud to your students. Take the sign off the doorknob when you have finished reading to your students. Put the "Do Not Disturb—Students Reading" sign on the outside doorknob of your classroom door just before students begin sustained silent reading (SSR) or other reading-for-pleasure time. Remove the sign when the reading-for-pleasure time is over.

When the "Do Not Disturb" signs are on your door, expect teachers, parents, administrators, and other students to honor these signs. Think of the powerful message you are communicating! You will want to make these signs immediately and begin proclaiming the importance of these reading activities by using them daily.

NOTE

These "Do Not Disturb" signs have such a powerful message that you may want to persuade *all* of the teachers in your building to use them. In this way every student in the building would be internalizing the message that the whole school thinks reading is so important, so great, so much fun that *NOTHING* can interrupt it. In addition, every classroom teacher would be encouraged to read aloud to his or her students and to provide time for students to read for pleasure in "real" books.

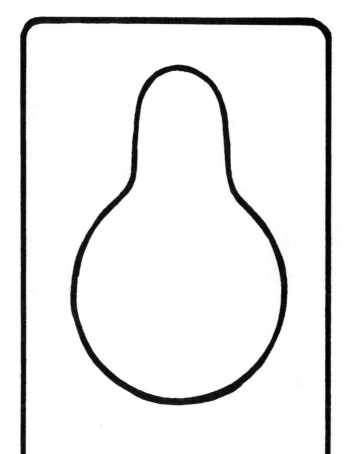

DO NOT DISTURB

Teacher reading aloud

**DO
NOT
DISTURB**

**Students
reading**

BOOK SCENE WINDOW SHADES

Do you have blah old dark or tan window shades in your classroom? How about turning those dreary window shades into bright, lively book advertisements?

Select several favorite books for your grade level. These books could be favorite books you read aloud to your students or super books most students at your grade level read independently and love. Each of the books you select should have good illustrations for you to enlarge and trace onto a window shade. (NOTE: Be sure you get your administrator's permission first before proceeding with this activity.)

Select the window shade you wish to decorate first. It might be the one in the center of the row of windows. Now select the book illustration you wish to paint on the window shade. Put the illustration in an opaque projector and project it onto the pulled-down window shade.* Position and focus the projector to obtain an appropriately sized, clear image of the illustration on the window shade.

Now, using white chalk, trace the illustration onto the window shade. Next, use acrylic paints to paint the picture onto the window shade.

The resulting painted illustration will delight you and your students each time you pull down that window shade. The book-promoting effect of your "masterpiece"— as well as the attractive, eye-catching appearance—will soon have you eagerly ready to decorate another and then another window shade with illustrations from other favorite books! Have fun making a "permanent improvement" in your classroom!

---

* If you do not have an opaque projector in your school, use a photocopier to make a transparency of the illustration. Then put the transparency on an overhead projector to project the illustration onto the window shade.

BOOKWORMS

Starting a bookworm with a body that grows as children read more and more books can serve as a reading incentive for students. As each child reads a book, he or she can add a segment to the bookworm's body. The body segments can be cut out of assorted colors of construction paper. Each time a child finishes reading a book, he or she prints the title of the book and his or her name on a construction paper body segment using a felt-tip marking pen. The bookworm head is then moved forward so that the new body segment can be placed right behind the head. The head and the body segment are then taped into position on the wall.

With eager readers, the bookworm's body can quickly grow around the room, right out the door, and down the hall!

WONDERFUL BOOKWORM VARIATIONS

If you are looking for something different and creative in place of the more common bookworm to engage your students in reading more prodigiously, you might want to consider some terrific bookworm variations.

VARIATION 1

Instead of a bookworm, consider a giraffe whose neck increases in length as the students read books. Begin by using a photocopier to make a transparency of the giraffe body and head patterns. Put the transparency onto an overhead projector and project it onto the wall. Cover that part of the wall with yellow bulletin board paper (kraft paper). Next, trace the outline of the giraffe onto the yellow paper. You will probably want to make the giraffe large. Take down the paper outline and trace over the outline with felt-tip markers. Color in where appropriate. Then cut out the giraffe and cut its head apart from its neck. Tape the giraffe to a wall in the classroom.

As the students read books, they can add segments to the giraffe's neck. Each segment added should indicate the name of the book read by the student and the name of the student. To add a neck segment, shift the giraffe's head forward and position the new neck segment right behind the head and tape in place. In this way the giraffe's head is moving forward each time a new book is read. As the students read more and more books, the giraffe's neck will grow longer and longer. Eventually it will grow around the room, out the door, and down the hall.

Your students will eagerly try to keep it growing and growing. The giraffe—with its growing neck—will soon be attracting the attention of other students in the school. Soon the whole school will be watching with admiration as the giraffe's neck lengthens.

VARIATION 2

Instead of a bookworm with a growing body or a giraffe with a lengthening neck, how about a friendly-looking giant with arms that keep growing as the students read more and more books. See the pattern outline for projecting and tracing.

VARIATION 3

Another terrific possibility is a daschund whose body grows and grows as the students read more and more books. See the pattern outline for projecting and tracing.

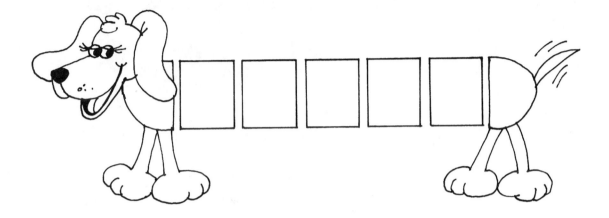

PENNANTS PROMOTING BOOKS

Let the students create pennants to promote books. Have the students design college-style pennants out of construction paper or kraft paper (bulletin board paper). The pennants should be designed to promote books, emphasizing the pleasure of reading or the importance of reading. Pennants can be hung on the classroom wall or hung in the school hallways.

43

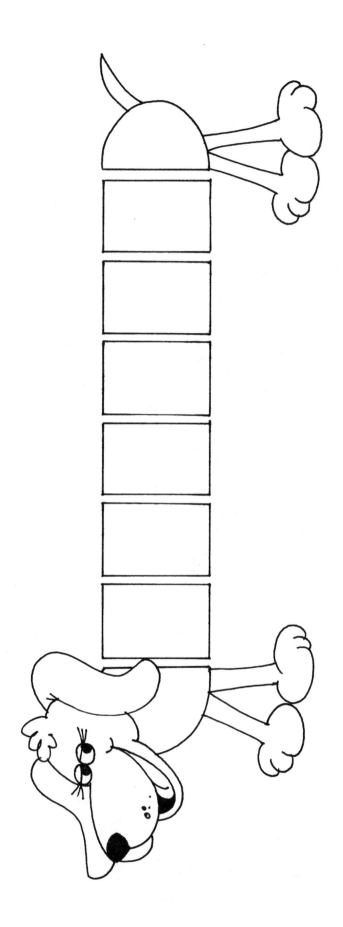

ENLARGE YOUR CLASSROOM LIBRARY

Would you like to add lots more books to your classroom library? Try looking for children's books at garage sales! Many garage sales have great children's books, both hardback and paperback, for sale from 10¢ to 30¢ each. These books usually have very little wear and tear; indeed, many are as good as new. Using a bit of selectivity, you can add many high-quality children's books to your grades 1-6 library at *very little cost*. Your students will love it and so will you!

"ROSES ARE RED" POEMS

Ask your students in grades 2-5 to write reading-promoting poems using the "Roses are red, violets are blue, . . ." poem pattern. Begin by writing the following poem on the chalkboard:

ॐ

Roses are red,

Violets are blue.

For always and forever,

I will love you.

ॐ

Read the poem aloud to the class. Then have the class read the poem aloud together once or twice so that they internalize its pattern and rhythm.

Next, you will want to model how to change the poem into a reading-promoting poem for the students. Begin by telling the students you're going to have some fun with this poem. Explain that you are going to write a new poem by changing the last two lines of the poem to make the new poem tell how great books are or what fun reading is.

On the chalkboard (or on chart paper) write the first two lines:

ॐ

Roses are red,

Violets are blue.

ॐ

Now, pause as though you are thinking. Say something like, "Let's see, I want to change the last two lines to say something about books or reading. Now, what will I say? I've got it!" Then write on the chalkboard (or chart paper) the final two lines of the verse, using lines of your choice from any of the examples given below or creating an original one of your own.

છ

Roses are red,

Violets are blue.

I love a good book,

And so will you!

છ

છ

Roses are red,

Violets are blue.

I love reading,

And so should you.

છ

છ

Roses are red,

Violets are blue.

You'll find lots of fun,

When you read the books I do.

છ

છ

Roses are red,

Violets are blue.

A book is the best present,

I can give to you.

છ

છ

Roses are red,

Violets are blue.

I love reading,

As you do, too.

છ

&

Roses are red,

Violets are blue.

You read to me,

And I'll read to you.

&

Next, create one or two more poems beginning with "Roses are red, violets are blue" and have the students brainstorm as a class the final two book- and/or reading-promoting lines. Write the class poem(s) on the chalkboard as the students think of the lines.

Now, have the students (individually or in pairs) write their own "Roses are red, violets are blue . . ." reading-promoting poems. After the students have shared their poems by reading them aloud to an appreciative audience, bind the poems together into a class book. Your students will enjoy reading and rereading their book of "ROSES ARE RED" POEMS that extols the importance or pleasure of books and reading.

VARIATION

If this activity is done near Valentine's Day, students can write their poems on red construction paper hearts. The hearts can then be mounted on a bulletin board to create a great display.

READING MOTIVATION BRACELETS
(GRADES 1-3)

Photocopy or duplicate the "Reading Motivation Bracelets" pattern. Using a paper cutter, cut the pages in half lengthwise to separate the bracelets and distribute a reading motivation bracelet to each student.

Have the students carefully color the pictures on the bracelet they have been given. Next, have the students cut out their bracelets. Then assist the students in taping their bracelets together on their wrists. (*OPTIONAL:* If desired, the bracelets can be laminated before the ends are taped together. This will increase the durability of the bracelets.)

Students will love wearing these motivation bracelets. At the same time, these bracelets will convey the message to students that books are fun and reading is enjoyable.

READING MOTIVATION BRACELETS

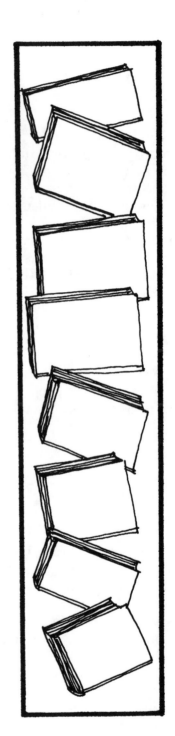

48

WORKSHEETS FOR PROMOTING READING

The following eleven worksheets can be used throughout the year to help promote reading by your students—both in the classroom and at home.

Favorite Reading Places

In each box below, draw a picture of yourself reading in one of your favorite places for reading. Beneath each picture identify that favorite spot for reading.

_____	_____	_____
_____	_____	_____

FAVORITE BOOKS I HAVE READ

NAME _____

Title _____

Author _____

Title _____

Author _____

Title _____

Author _____

Title _____

Author _____

Title _____

Author _____

Title _____

Author _____

BOOKSTORE . . . AND MORE

Imagine that you own a bookstore. You want to place an advertisement in the newspaper. Design your advertisement, encouraging people to buy and read books—especially ones from your bookstore!

BOOK TIME . . . ANYTIME!

List 20 super times to pick up a good book, lean back, and enjoy reading. Begin with the obvious best times, then turn your imagination loose and think up a lot more great times to read a book!

1. _____
2. _____
3. _____
4. _____
5. _____
6. _____
7. _____
8. _____
9. _____
10. _____
11. _____
12. _____
13. _____
14. _____
15. _____
16. _____
17. _____
18. _____
19. _____
20. _____

Compare your list with the lists of your classmates.

WANT LIST

Books I want to read soon:

1. _____
2. _____
3. _____
4. _____
5. _____
6. _____

Topics I would like to read about:

1. _____
   _____
2. _____
   _____
3. _____
   _____
4. _____
   _____
5. _____
   _____
6. _____
   _____

NAME _____

BUMPER STICKER FUN

Design two bumper stickers that emphasize the pleasure or the importance of reading.

DESIGN READING BOOKMARKS

Design four different bookmarks that will make other people want to read. Include pictures and slogans. Color the bookmarks to make them even more interesting!

Cut out your bookmarks. Trade bookmarks with your friends, if you wish. Then use the bookmarks!

CREATE A T-SHIRT

Design a T-shirt that tells people books are great and reading is fun!

More shirt ideas? Trace the shirt outline onto another sheet of paper and design another reading T-shirt!

THREE CHEERS FOR READING!

Books are super!
Books are great!
Grab a book and read today!

Books are winners and worth cheering about. In the space below, write three different cheers for books and reading.

Select your best cheer and teach it to other members of your class!

58

READING RADIO ANNOUNCEMENT

Write a 30- to 60-second radio announcement emphasizing the fun of reading or the importance of reading.

_____

_____

_____

_____

_____

_____

_____

_____

_____

_____

_____

_____

_____

_____

_____

_____

_____

_____

FOR FUN . . .

Tape record your reading radio announcement.
Then play the tape recording for the rest of the class.

BOOKS ARE FUN

Write a letter to a friend convincing him or her of the fun of reading books. Use the back of this sheet if you need more space to write.

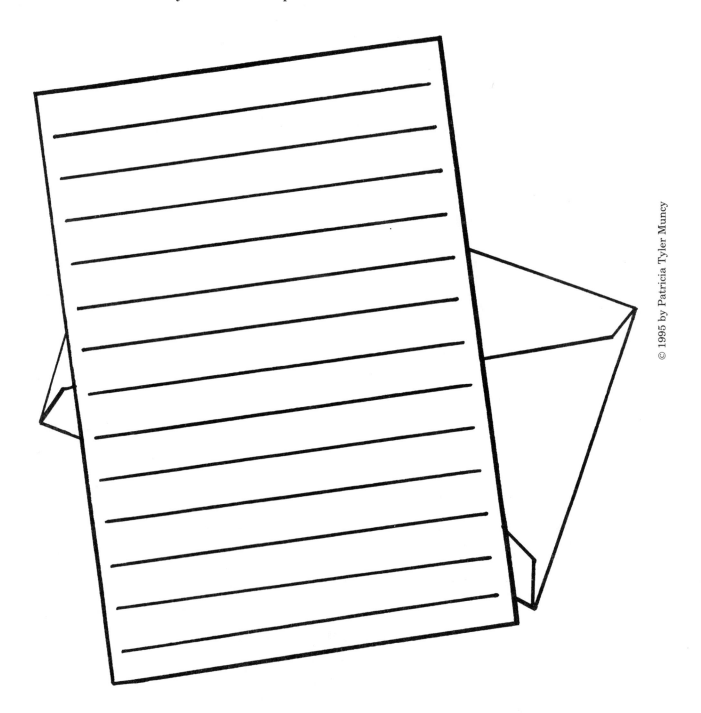

Section 4

Seasonal Book-Related Activities

HALLOWEEN BOOK CHARACTER COSTUME PARTY

Have a book character costume party for which the students are asked to wear costumes to school on a specified day. However, instead of wearing the usual Halloween costumes, ask the students to dress up as favorite book characters. Brainstorm together some book character possibilities to get students' ideas flowing. Tell the students they should plan on wearing their costumes the entire school day.

Send a note home, well in advance of the specified day, telling parents about the book character costume party and asking that they help their child prepare for the costume party. Point out to the parents that the costumes can range from very simple to more elaborate, but they should reflect, in some way, the character to be represented. For example, Tom Sawyer could be depicted by a child wearing old jeans and a shirt with a shirttail hanging out and carrying an empty, old paint bucket with a paintbrush.

On the costume party day, have special activities such as a class guessing game called "What Character Am I?", a book character parade through other classes in the school, and a book character Halloween party with Halloween cookies and punch.

You may wish to bring a camera to school and take lots of pictures of your little book characters. These pictures can then be placed in a Class Book-Character Picture Album for students to look through and enjoy throughout the year.

NOTE: It is important that you also dress up as a favorite book character! So, put on your thinking cap and come up with a terrific costume idea for yourself.

SHRINK-PLASTIC BOOK CHARACTER HOLIDAY ORNAMENTS

With this activity students will make beautiful holiday ornaments depicting their favorite book characters.

To implement this activity, you will need to order shrink plastic from:

K & B Innovations, Inc.
P.O. Box 66
Brookfield, WI 53005
Phone: 414-966-7550

You will be ordering their product called "Shrinky Dinks Refill Pack." A 20-sheet pack will cost approximately $6.00. A 200-sheet pack will cost approximately $50.00. Before ordering the shrink plastic, call or write to check the current price. To determine the quantity you will need to order, figure that each student will need a half to whole sheet of plastic. You will also want to order a number of extra sheets so you can experiment ahead of time and create some sample book-character ornaments to show the students. You will also want to have a few extra sheets of shrink plastic just in case some students mess theirs up and need to start with new plastic.

Making the shrink-plastic ornaments is really very easy. Students draw or trace pictures of book characters on the plastic. When the plastic is baked in a 300° oven for 30 seconds to 2 minutes, the shrink plastic shrinks to approximately one-third size. At the same time the plastic thickens and the colors of the drawing intensify. The finished product is a delightful miniaturized version of the original.

To begin, use a permanent black, fine-line Sharpie® Pen and trace the ornament pattern outline onto each sheet of shrink plastic, one sheet for each student. For younger students, you will probably want to do this yourself. Older students can trace the ornament outline themselves. If you are going to have older students do them themselves, you will probably want to make a number of photocopies of the ornament outline so students can quickly and easily make the outline on their sheets of shrink plastic. You will also need a number of black Sharpie® Pens so that the process can move along quickly.

Next, have each student select a favorite book character, then draw or trace that character onto the matt-finished side of the shrink-plastic ornament. Permanent fine-line markers and good quality colored pencils will work well in drawing and coloring the book characters on the shrink plastic. (Do NOT use crayons or non-permanent ink marking pens.) Non-colored areas will shrink frosted. Therefore, when white is desired, the student should color the area with a white colored pencil.

Students should be sure to print the book title on their ornaments so that the book characters will be easily recognizable to everyone. Next, the students cut out their ornaments with scissors and, using a hand-held hole punch, punch a hole at the top of their ornaments.

Now the items are ready for shrinking. The shrinking can be done in a toaster oven or a regular oven. (NOTE: A microwave oven will *NOT* shrink the shrink plastic.) Preheat the oven to 300°. Place the shrink plastic piece(s) on a

non-stick cookie sheet or a regular cookie sheet lined with aluminum foil. Place in the oven for approximately two minutes. The shrink plastic pieces will curl and twist as they bake. However, they will lie almost flat when they have finished shrinking. To flatten any shrink-plastic pieces that do not come out totally flat, remove them from the oven and put some weight on them to hold the pieces flat as they cool.

It works best to only shrink two or three pieces at a time just in case you need to put some weight on the shrunken pieces to flatten them further. If you try to shrink too many at a time, some of the pieces that might need further flattening may be too cool by the time you get to them.

When the shrink-plastic ornaments have cooled, the students can thread a piece of red ribbon through the hole at the top of the ornament, then tie a small bow so that there is a loop of ribbon with a small bow on top. The loop of ribbon can be used for hanging the ornament on a Christmas tree branch, a Hanukkah bush, or an Easter egg tree.

Students will be delighted with these ornaments. You may wish to use the ornaments to decorate a classroom tree, then allow the students to take their ornaments home the last day before a holiday vacation.

These book character ornaments might become treasured family keepsakes that will be enjoyed holiday after holiday for many, many years.

PATTERN FOR SHRINK-PLASTIC BOOK CHARACTER ORNAMENT

(Pattern can be reduced, if desired.)

HANUKKAH GIFT EXCHANGES

Hanukkah is a Jewish holiday that is observed for eight days in early December. During this holiday celebration Jewish children often receive a small gift each day at dinnertime.

Tell your students a little about the Jewish celebration of Hanukkah and about the practice of Jewish children receiving small gifts at dinner during the eight days of Hanukkah. Tell the students that they are going to prepare small gifts to give each other at lunchtime on each of the school days during Hanukkah.

Let the students draw names of classmates, a different student name for each of the school days during Hanukkah. Next, have them make gifts for the students whose names they have drawn. Give the students the following gift choices:

- Write a story for your friend. Illustrate it if you wish. Then make an attractive book cover for it.
- Make a bookmark or a set of bookmarks.
- Make an ornament or decoration with a favorite book character on it.
- Make a placemat with pictures of favorite book characters drawn on it. Laminate the placemat.
- Create some note paper with book character drawings as decorations.
- Check out one of your favorite books from the school library. Put a note inside of it telling what a great book it is and asking that the recipient return it to you when he or she has finished reading it so that you can take it back to the library.
- Other ideas? Feel free to create other gifts as long as they are book or book character related in some way.

Provide assorted wrapping paper, scissors, and transparent tape for students to use in wrapping each of the little gifts. Just before lunch each day, the students can put their gifts on the desks of the receiving students. The students can take their unopened presents to the cafeteria and open them when they sit down to eat their lunches.

FAVORITE BOOK HOLIDAY ORNAMENTS

This activity promotes the love of books. You'll need:

small-size plastic margarine tub lids (one per child),
heavy white art paper,
several compasses for drawing circles,
paper cutter,
white all-purpose glue,
hole punch,
colored pencils (assorted colors),
Flair® Pens (assorted colors),
yarn,
scissors,
containers of red, green, and gold glitter (optional),
red and green rickrack available from craft/sewing stores (optional)

PREPARATION

A couple of weeks before starting this activity, ask students to bring in one or more plastic lids from the small-size margarine tubs. When students have brought in enough margarine lids so that each student can have a lid, you are ready to begin.

Give each student a margarine tub lid and a half sheet of heavy white art paper. Have students use compasses to draw onto their pieces of white art paper a circle that will fit inside the ridge on the top of their margarine tub lid. Then have the students cut out their paper circle.

Next, have the students think back over the books they have read or that have been read to them and bring to mind his or her all-time favorite book. Using a Flair® Pen or other fine-line marker, have each student print the title of that all-time favorite book onto his or her white paper circle. Next, using colored pencils or crayons, have them draw a picture on the paper circle to represent the book. The picture might be of the main character, setting, or an exciting event in the story.

Next, the students should glue the circles to the top of their plastic margarine tub lids, then punch a hole with a hole punch so that the holiday ornament can be hung when it is finished.

The next step is optional, but very nice and results in more eye-catching ornaments. Have the students glue rickrack or glitter onto the rim of the margarine tub lid.

Finally, have students cut a piece of yarn, thread it through the hole in the lid, and tie it so as to form a loop that can be used to hang the ornament. Now the holiday ornament is completed and ready to use on a classroom holiday tree and/or to take home for the family tree.

HAPPY NEW YEAR ENVELOPES

On New Year's Day, Chinese children receive a red envelope containing a gift of money. With this in mind, you may wish to give each of your students a special New Year gift, Chinese style, their first day back in school after New Year's Day.

Prepare five "coupons" for each student in the class. The coupons entitle the students to free reading time in place of doing an in-class homework assignment. Next, you will need to make red envelopes in which to stuff the five coupons.

You can make red envelopes out of red construction paper. Take a regular envelope and carefully pick the glued flaps open. Next, place the envelope, with all of the flaps spread open, on a sheet of red construction paper. Trace around the spread-open envelope. Cut along the traced outline on the construction paper. Next, fold the construction paper envelope flaps into regular envelope position. Then using rubber cement, glue the flaps in the same manner the original envelope had been glued. Voilá, a red envelope!

You will need to make a red envelope for each student. Next, stuff each envelope with five coupons.

On the first school day after New Year's Day, tell the students a little about how Chinese people celebrate the New Year. Tell them about Chinese children receiving red envelopes containing a gift of money. Explain to them that you have a special red envelope for each of them. Explain that while their envelopes do not contain money, they do contain something even better than money. Tell them the envelopes contain free reading coupons entitling them to free reading time in place of doing in-class homework assignments. Distribute a red envelope "gift" to each student.

To "cash in" a coupon, the student must give you one of his or her free reading time coupons and specify to you which assignment the student is replacing with free reading. Make a note on the back of the coupon indicating the assignment the student is excused from doing. The student then goes to his or her desk and enjoys a free reading time!

FAVORITE BOOK CHARACTERS

Distribute a copy of the "Favorite Book Characters" activity sheet to each student. Ask the students to think about the great books they have read or that have been read to them over the years and to bring to mind their all-time favorite book characters. Have them write the names of those favorite book characters on the valentines on the activity sheet. Then, beneath the name of each character, the students can write the title of the book in which that character was found.

When they have filled in the book character names and book titles on the valentines, the students can outline the valentines with red colored pencils or crayons, then lightly color the inside of each valentine. The completed "Favorite Book Characters" activity sheets can be displayed for other students' viewing.

NAME

FAVORITE BOOK CHARACTERS

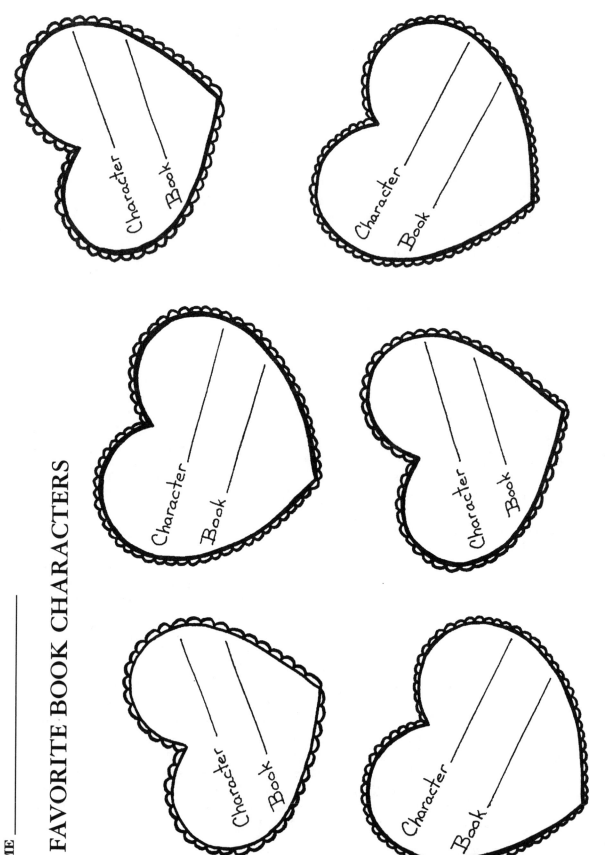

"EGGS-CITING" BOOKS

This book report activity center motivates students to read books. You'll need:

large Easter basket
green Easter "grass"
plastic eggs in assorted colors (at least 1 egg per child in the room plus one
    for the teacher, more if desired)
a stuffed rabbit (optional)
sheets of white duplicator paper
paper cutter
display table
5″ × 20″ piece of yellow posterboard
black fine-line felt-tip permanent marker
black wide-line felt-tip permanent marker
transparent tape.

PREPARATION

Put Easter grass into the Easter basket and place the basket in the center of a table. (*Optional:* Position a stuffed rabbit near the Easter basket.) Place a permanent fine-line black marker beside the basket. Put plastic eggs, individually and in groups of two or three, around the table. Cut thirty to forty 3″ × 5″ pieces of paper and place them in a stack on the table. Using the black wide-line marker, print "EGGS-CITING" BOOKS on the 5″ × 20″ piece of yellow posterboard, and tape this activity title sign onto the table.

PROCEDURE

Have students read library books for pleasure. Then, when a student finishes reading a book, have him or her select a plastic egg and, using the fine-line permanent marker, print the title of the book, the author, and the student's own name on the surface of the plastic egg. Next, have the student take one of the 3″ × 5″ pieces of paper and write the title of the book and the author's name on the front side of the paper. On the back side of the paper, have the student write why he or she thinks other students would like to read the book. The student then folds this paper, puts it inside the plastic egg, and places the egg in the Easter basket. Next, the student displays his or her book by standing it up on the table.

After a number of eggs have been completed and the corresponding books have been placed on display on the table, encourage the students to look at each other's eggs and consider reading some of the student-recommended books. Point out to the students that only one egg should be completed for each title. However, if other students read a book for which an egg has already been made, those students should add their names beneath the first student's name to indicate that they, too, have read the book.

As students get caught up in this reading motivation activity, you may wish to add more plastic eggs and another Easter basket.

NOTE

You should be reading children's books and filling out eggs right along with the students.

Section 5

CREATIVE
BOOK
REPORTS

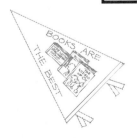

DESIGN A BOOK SCENE POSTCARD

Designing a book scene postcard is a terrific alternative to a boring book report. Cut sheets of white or manila-colored tagboard into cards 4 1/4" × 6" in size. You will need one per student plus a couple of extras. (Use the extras to create several sample book scene postcards to show the students.)

Instead of the traditional book report, each student will draw and color a scene from the book he or she has read on the front of the "postcard." The illustration should include nice detail and be neatly colored using fine-line pens and good quality colored pencils.

On the back of the postcard, the student draws a vertical line dividing the card in half. Next, on the upper left section of the back of the postcard, each student identifies the scene pictured on the front of his or her postcard and states the title and author of the book. Next, each student addresses his or her postcard to a friend or relative in the normal manner. Finally, each student will use the usual postcard message area on the left side of the card to tell his or her friend or relative about the book.

The completed book scene postcards can be mailed as real postcards or can be put into a postcard album and placed on a display table. The album will display both the front and back of each postcard. The students will then enjoy leafing through the album and looking at each other's book scene postcards and reading the information written about each of the books in the message section of the postcards.

Front

Back

BOOK PENNANTS

How about lining the walls of your classroom or the hallways of your school with pennants representing books your students have read? This activity can be a great alternative to deadly, boring oral book reports and the dreaded written book reports. Or, this activity can simply be a reading-incentive activity to encourage students to read, read, read. Or, better yet, it could serve both purposes.

Visualize the long narrow triangular college pennants made out of felt. Now, visualize something very similar made out of bright colored bulletin board paper and representing books instead of colleges. Picture in your mind's eye an illustration of a book character drawn at the wider end of the triangle and the title of the book boldly printed next to it.

Now visualize your students eagerly reading one book after another and creating book pennants for each one, with the objective of having a colorful series of book pennants displayed side by side around the classroom proclaiming the books they have read.

At a fourth grade or higher level, this activity is too good to skip! To implement, simply make a pennant pattern out of posterboard. Students will trace this pattern onto the bulletin board paper whenever they are ready to create a book pennant. Next, the student will cut the pennant out of the bulletin board paper. Then, he or she will be ready to complete the pennant by drawing a picture of the book character and printing the title of the book on the pennant.

NOTE: Providing students with a posterboard pattern to trace around will result in all of the student pennants being the same size and shape. This will result in a very attractive book pennant display.

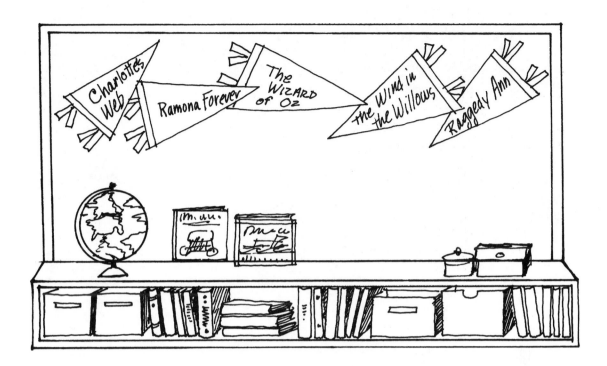

CHALK SCENES

Let children draw chalk scenes from books as an alternative to book reports. Give each child a sheet of heavy white paper. Using a sponge and a pan of water, have each child moisten the surface of the paper thoroughly. Next, using colored chalk, let each child draw a picture of a favorite scene from a good book. The title of the book should be printed neatly across the page, either with chalk or after the page has dried using a fine-line marker.

Using colored chalk on wet paper will result in brighter chalk colors and chalk pictures less easily smeared when dry. To select scenes to draw, the children will most certainly have read the books they are depicting. Therefore, written reports on the books should be unnecessary.

The completed and dry pictures can be mounted on an attractive construction paper background. The pictures can then be displayed in a prime location for viewing and enjoying.

DIORAMAS

Letting students make dioramas of scenes with characters from books they have read can be another good book report alternative.

Let each child make an interesting diorama using a shoebox or other appropriate size box. Tempera paints, modeling clay, twigs, small stones, and other appropriate items and materials can be used to make the scenes. Book characters for the scenes can be made from cardboard, pipe cleaners, clothespins, clay, yarn, etc. The possibilities are unlimited. With time, patience, creativity and imagination, the resulting dioramas will be exciting testimonials of books read and enjoyed.

Section 6

CONTESTS FOR PROMOTING READING

READING ADVERTISEMENT CONTEST

This may well become your favorite reading-promoting contest. Indeed, this one is so good you may want to do it annually! In this contest, students create reading advertisements emphasizing the pleasure of books and/or the importance of reading. The winning advertisements are then printed as real advertisements in the local newspaper! The contest can be implemented district-wide, grades 1-12. You may choose to set it up for just your school or for your entire school district.

BACKGROUND INFORMATION FOR CONTEST COORDINATOR(S)

To implement this contest you will first need to talk to the local newspaper editor, explain the contest, and ask if the editor would print the winning reading-promoting advertisements as real advertisements free of charge in the newspaper. Many newspapers will gladly support the contest in this way because they want students to develop into good adult readers. Therefore, newspapers are interested in supporting activities that encourage reading. In addition, printing the students' reading advertisements in the newspaper is good public relations for the newspaper as well as good public relations for the school.

After the newspaper editor has indicated the willingness to print the winning advertisements free of charge, you will need to determine how many winning advertisements the editor will be willing to print within a week or two-week period of time. Once this has been established, you are ready to proceed.

Determine the following as you plan and prepare to implement your READING ADVERTISEMENT CONTEST:

1. Will the contest be just for your school or will it include other schools within your school district? If so, which ones?

2. What grade levels do you want to include in the contest?

3. When will you want to distribute fliers announcing the contest?

4. How much time should there be between the time you distribute fliers announcing the contest and the contest entry deadline?

5. When will be your contest entry deadline?

6. Who will be designated to receive the reading advertisement contest entries?

7. Who will be the contest judges?

8. Who will be responsible for getting the illustrations on the winning advertisements "print ready" for the newspaper?

Once you have thought through the answers to these questions, you are ready to prepare a flier announcing the READING ADVERTISEMENT CONTEST. Use the sample READING ADVERTISEMENT CONTEST announcement to help you develop your flier.

Once the winning advertisements have been selected, someone will need to get the advertisements "print ready" for the newspaper. The students will have used various colors of crayons, colored pencils, and/or fine-line markers in creating their advertisements. Some of the colors they have used will not show up clearly when printed in the newspaper. Therefore, you will need to provide the newspaper with a clear black-and-white copy of each advertisement.

The best way to obtain a black-and-white copy and to determine what work, if any, you will need to do to the advertisements is simply to make a photocopy of each of them on a photocopy machine. Examine the photocopy to see what "touching up" you may need to do. You may also want to experiment with the lighter/darker adjustment on the photocopier to see if you can get better quality copies of some of the advertisements.

The photocopies of the advertisements will tell you what you need to do to ready each advertisement for the newspaper. Do the fixing up right on the photocopies of the advertisements. Use a black Flair® pen to go over any lines that need to be darkened or improved on the photocopy of each advertisement. Use a black colored pencil to provide shading or smooth out shading. Liquid Paper® can also be used for needed touch-ups. You may also need to improve somewhat the quality of lettering on the advertisements. You need to be careful that you do not "improve" the advertisements so much that the advertisements become yours instead of the students'. On the other hand, you do want them to show up well when they appear in the newspaper.

The photocopies of the advertisements will become the black-and-white, print-ready copy you will provide the newspaper. Therefore, be sure that you print clearly the student's name, grade, and school on the back of each reading advertisement. The newspaper will want to include this information beneath each advertisement when they print the advertisements.

Students, parents, and the public in general will thoroughly enjoy seeing the reading advertisements in the newspaper!

ANNOUNCING

READING ADVERTISEMENT CONTEST

Students in grades *(insert grade levels)* are invited to enter the *(insert name of cooperating newspaper and name of school or school district)* READING ADVERTISEMENT CONTEST.

<u>READING ADVERTISEMENT CONTEST RULES</u>:

1. The contestant will submit a reading-promoting advertisement on a sheet of white 8 1/2" × 11" paper.

2. The advertisement should emphasize the pleasure of reading and/or the importance of reading.

3. The advertisement should be designed <u>on white paper using primarily black or dark-colored markers or crayons, so that winning entries will print clearly in the newspaper</u>.

4. The contestant's name, grade level, teacher, and school *(if the contest is district wide)* must be written legibly on the back of the advertisement.

5. All entries should be submitted to *(insert name of individual and location)* <u>no later than *(insert date—day, month, year)*</u>.

6. Entries will be judged on the morning of *(insert date)*.

7. <u>Any entry shall be the work of the student submitting it</u>.

8. All entries become the property of *(insert name of school/district)*.

9. Winners will be determined by a committee of judges.

<u>CONTEST PRIZES</u>:

1. A total of *(number)* winning reading advertisements will be selected from entries from grades *(insert grade levels)*. Selection of the winning entries will be distributed over all grade levels so that younger students are not competing with older students.

2. Thanks to the cooperation of *(insert name of cooperating newspaper)*, <u>the winning advertisements will be printed as real advertisements in the newspaper *(insert dates)*</u>.

DESIGN-A-BOOKMARK CONTEST

This wonderful reading-promoting contest is too good to pass up! The winning entries are printed as real bookmarks and distributed to the students within the school or school district. This is a great contest to consider implementing district-wide, grades 2-12.

BACKGROUND INFORMATION FOR CONTEST COORDINATOR(S)

Begin by reading the sample DESIGN-A-BOOKMARK CONTEST announcement to get an overview of the contest. To implement this contest you will probably want to find a company within your community that will be willing to underwrite the cost of a printing company printing the winning bookmarks.

Before contacting a local business for financial support of this activity, contact one or more local printing companies to determine likely printing costs. Discuss costs in terms of the printing company setting the type for the words on the bookmarks and printing the bookmarks on assorted colors of coverstock or similar weight paper.

Once you have obtained the money commitment for the printing of the bookmarks, you are ready to proceed with the planning and implementation of your contest. You will need to determine the following as you plan your DESIGN-A-BOOKMARK CONTEST:

1. Will the contest be just for your school or will it include other schools within your district? If so, which ones?

2. What grade levels do you want to include in the contest?

3. How many GRAND WINNING bookmark entries do you plan to have printed as real bookmarks?

4. What grade-level groups will be judged together?

5. When do you want to distribute fliers announcing the contest?

6. How much time should there be between the time you distribute the fliers announcing the contest and the contest entry deadline?

7. When will be your contest entry deadline?

8. Who will be designated to receive the bookmark contest entries?

9. Who will be the contest judges?

10. Who will be responsible for getting the illustrations on the winning bookmarks "print ready" for the printers?

Once you have thought through the answers to these questions, you are ready to prepare a flier announcing the DESIGN-A-BOOKMARK CONTEST. Use the sample DESIGN-A-BOOKMARK CONTEST announcement to help you in developing your flier.

Once the winning bookmarks have been selected, someone will need to get the illustrations on the bookmarks "print ready" for the printer. This will take a little time. The students will have used various colors of crayon, colored pencils, and/or felt-tip markers in creating their bookmarks, and some of the colors may not be picked up by the printer the print company will use. You will need to provide the printer with a clear black-and-white copy of each of the bookmarks.

The best way to obtain a black-and-white copy and to determine what, if any, work you may need to do to the illustrations on each of the bookmarks is simply to make a photocopy of each bookmark on a photocopy machine. Then examine the photocopy to see what "touching up" you may need to do. You may also want to experiment with the lighter/darker adjustment on the photocopier to see if you can get better quality copies of some of the bookmarks.

The photocopies of the bookmarks will tell you what you need to do to ready each bookmark for the print company. Do the fixing-up right on the photocopies of the bookmarks. Use a black Flair® pen to go over any lines that need to be darkened or improved. Use a black colored pencil to provide shading or smooth out shading on any of the photocopies. Liquid Paper® can also be used for needed touch-ups. Do not worry about the quality of lettering on the bookmarks on which you are working because the print company will provide the lettering for the words on the bookmarks.

The "improved" photocopies of the bookmarks will become the black-and-white, print-ready copy you will provide the print company. Therefore, be sure to print lightly in pencil on the back of each bookmark the student's name, grade level, and school. Take the photocopy, print-ready bookmarks, along with the students' original bookmarks, to the print company. Be sure to ask the printer to include in small print at the bottom of each bookmark the name of the student who created the bookmark as well as his or her grade level and school. You may also wish to have the printer include a line saying "Printed courtesy of *(name of the company paying for the printing of the bookmarks)*."

The colorful bookmarks you will receive from the printing company will be of excellent quality and truly delightful. Everyone will enjoy this contest and its results!

ANNOUNCING

DESIGN-A-BOOKMARK CONTEST

Students in grades *(insert grade levels)* are invited to enter the *(insert name of school or school district)* DESIGN-A-BOOKMARK CONTEST.

CONTEST RULES:

1. The contestant will design a bookmark on a <u>2 1/4" × 8" piece of white paper</u>.

2. The bookmark should be designed to <u>emphasize in some way the fun of reading and/or the importance of reading</u>. Some possibilities might include reading-oriented illustrations, slogans, or poems.

3. Crayons, colored pencils, felt-tip markers, etc., can be used to add color to illustrations.

4. The contestant's name, grade level, teacher, and school should be written lightly but legibly on the back of the bookmark.

5. All entries should be submitted to *(insert name of individual and location)* <u>no later than</u> <u>*(insert date—day, month, year)*</u>.

6. Entries will be judged *(insert date)*.

7. ANY ENTRY SHALL BE THE WORK OF THE STUDENT SUBMITTING IT.

8. Entries will not be returned.

9. Winners will be determined by a committee of judges.

CONTEST PRIZES:

1. *(Insert number)* bookmarks will be judged to be the GRAND WINNERS—1 winner in each of the following grade-level groups: *(insert grade-level groups, perhaps grades 2-4, 5-6, 7-8, and grades 9-12)*.

2. Thanks to the *(insert name of contest-sponsoring company)* the *(insert number of winning bookmarks to be selected)* GRAND-WINNING bookmarks will be printed as real bookmarks and distributed to all of the school libraries in our school district for free distribution to all students in our district. The bookmarks will also be distributed through the *(indicate name of local public library)*!

READING BUTTON SLOGAN CONTEST

For this contest students design reading-promoting button artwork. The GRAND WINNING button is then reproduced as a metal-backed, pin-on badge-type button.

BACKGROUND INFORMATION FOR CONTEST COORDINATOR(S)

To get an overview of the contest, read the sample READING BUTTON SLOGAN CONTEST announcement flier. To implement this contest it is essential that you have access to BADGE A MINIT™ button-making equipment as well as a quantity of button part sets (each set includes a clear plastic cover, metal front, and metal pin back). If your school or school district does not have the needed equipment and button parts, they can be purchased from:

Badge a Minit
348 North 30th Road
Box 800
LaSalle, IL 61301
Phone: 1-800-223-4103 for a free catalog

Next, you will need to decide how you will reproduce the winning button artwork (slogan and illustration) that will be snapped into the button parts. Are you going to reproduce the button artwork on a photocopier, then have a committee of teachers color with colored pencils the artwork on each copy before it is cut out and snapped into the button parts? Or, are you going to take the winning button artwork to the printing company and have it reproduced in color in the quantity needed? Having the printing company reproduce the button artwork is definitely an easier way to go, but it is also more expensive. Both ways of reproducing the artwork will work, so your budget and the time commitment of the teachers involved will be the deciding factors.

If you want to add in the awarding of free hamburger certificates to the GRAND WINNER and a number of good runner-ups, you will need to contact a local fast-food restaurant, explain the contest, and ask if they would be willing to contribute free hamburger certificates for contest prizes.

Once these important contest components are in place, proceed with the planning and implementation of your contest. You are now ready to determine the following:

1. Will the contest be just for your school or will it include other schools within your school district? If so, which ones?

2. What grade levels do you want to include in the contest?

3. When do you want to distribute fliers announcing the contest?

4. When will the contest entry deadline be?

5. Who will be designated to receive the READING BUTTON SLOGAN CONTEST entries?

6. What quantity of the GRAND-WINNING reading buttons will be made and how will they be distributed within the school or school district?

7. Who will be the judges for the contest?

8. Who will be responsible for cutting out the artwork and snapping it into the button parts?

9. Who will be responsible for distributing the free hamburger certificates to the GRAND WINNER and the runners-up?

The winning reading button will create quite a stir among the teachers and many of the students! You may want to make a number of extra ones and sell them for $1.00 each to teachers and students.

(Sample READING BUTTON SLOGAN CONTEST announcement. Adapt or modify to explain your contest.)

ANNOUNCING

READING BUTTON SLOGAN CONTEST

Students in grades *(insert grade levels)* are invited to enter the *(insert name of school or school district)* READING BUTTON SLOGAN CONTEST.

CONTEST RULES:

1. The contestant will submit a slogan on a circular piece of paper that is provided. (<u>Button circles are provided on the attached page. Reproduce, cut page into quarters and distribute to contestants.</u>)

2. The slogan should emphasize the fun of reading for pleasure and/or the importance of reading.

3. An illustration can be incorporated into the button design.

4. The contestant's name, grade level, teacher's name, and school should be written lightly but legibly on the back of the entry.

5. All entries should be submitted to *(insert name of staff member to receive entries)* no later than *(insert date)*.

6. Entries will be judged the week of *(insert date)*.

7. Any entry shall be the work of the student submitting it.

8. All entries become the property of *(insert name of school or school district)* and will not be returned.

9. The winners will be determined by a committee of judges.

CONTEST PRIZES:

1. The button judged to be the GRAND WINNER will be printed as a real button (metal badge-type button) and will be distributed on a limited basis.

2. The GRAND WINNER will receive five of the buttons containing his or her slogan.

3. Other winners at each grade level will receive certificates for free hamburgers at *(insert name of cooperating restaurant)*.

READING BUTTON SLOGAN CONTEST
Button Circles

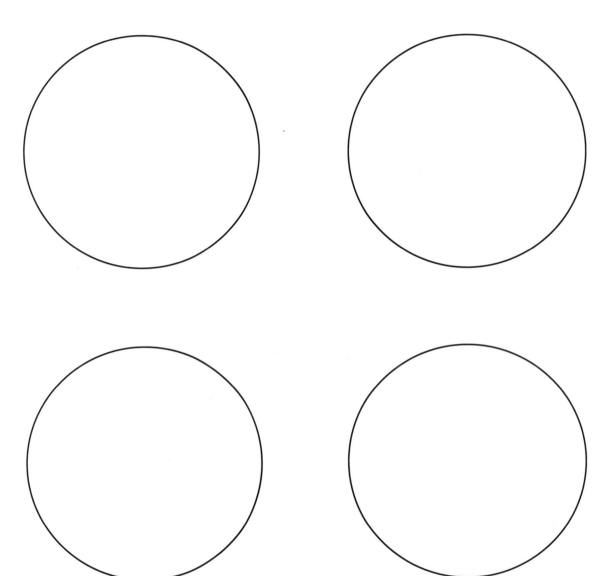

WRITE-A-READING-POEM CONTEST

This is another super contest that emphasizes the pleasure and importance of reading that can be set up for your building or entire school district.

BACKGROUND INFORMATION FOR CONTEST COORDINATOR(S)

To implement this contest, begin by reading the sample flier announcing the contest. The sample flier will give you a quick picture of the contest. It is now up to you to set up your WRITE-A-READING-POEM CONTEST.

First, it is important to decide whether this will be a building-wide or school district-wide contest and what grade levels will be included. The contest works well for grades 1-12. If you are including grades 1 and 2 in the contest, you will want to include the option of class or reading-group poem entries from those grade levels.

In setting up the contest you need to plan a timeline for distributing fliers announcing the contest and a realistic final date for reading-poem entries to be submitted. A reasonable deadline for entries might be 3-4 weeks from the time you plan to distribute the fliers announcing the contest. You will also have to decide to whom the reading-poem contest entries are going to be submitted so that you can include that information on your contest flier.

Next, you will want to select the day(s) the entries will be judged and actually select the judges for the contest. The judges must be individuals who can judge the entries in an unbiased manner. The judges might be several school-district administrators, some members of the community, or a couple of teachers from another building or district. You will only need three or four judges.

For this contest it is logical to have the winning entries printed into a booklet of winning reading poems. It is a wise idea to say that "a number of winning poems will be selected from each of the grade levels" involved in the contest. (See item 1 under CONTEST PRIZES on the sample contest announcement.) If you specify in the announcement a specific number of winning poems you intend to select from each grade level, you will probably find it hard to stay with that number. You may find at one or two grade levels there are only a few good poems and at other grade levels there are a number of really outstanding poems. You will want to word the flier announcement so that you have the flexibility of selecting poems that are indeed deserving of selection as winning entries!

Finally, you will need to decide how many copies of the resulting booklet of reading poems will be distributed. (See Rules 2-4 on the sample announcement flier for some possibilities.) And, you will need to determine who will actually be responsible for taking the winning poems and having them printed into a booklet.

If you want to include additional prizes of recognition for students whose poems are selected as winners, feel free to incorporate those into the contest you are designing and into the flier announcing the contest.

The teachers and students will enjoy this reading-promoting contest and so will the contest judges. In addition, proud parents of students whose poems are included in the booklet will be clamoring for extra copies to send to relatives!

NOTE

Be careful not to set the criteria for "winning" so high that only a very few reading poems are selected. Keep in mind the real purpose of the contest is to make students feel good about reading *and* their reading poems. Therefore, the judges will want to select all of the *good* reading poem entries as winners for inclusion in the booklet!

ANNOUNCING

WRITE-A-READING-POEM CONTEST

Students in grades *(insert grade levels)* are invited to enter the *(insert name of school or district)* WRITE-A-READING-POEM CONTEST.

<u>CONTEST RULES:</u>

1. The contestant will <u>write an original poem emphasizing in some way the fun of reading and/or the importance of reading</u>.

2. All entries should be written (or typed) neatly on a sheet of tablet paper, notebook paper, or photocopier paper.

3. The contestant may add illustrations to his or her entry, if desired. However, the entries will be judged on the basis of the poem itself.

4. Grades 1-2 have the option of submitting either an individually developed poem, small group developed poem, or a class developed poem.

5. In grades *(designate grade levels)*, EACH POEM MUST BE THE ORIGINAL WORK OF THE INDIVIDUAL STUDENT SUBMITTING IT.

6. The contestant's name, grade level, and teacher must be written legibly on the back of the entry.

7. In the case of a class entry (grades 1 and 2), the grade level and teacher must be written legibly on the back of the entry.

8. All entries must be submitted to *(insert name of individual and location)* <u>no later than</u> *(insert date—day, month, year)*.

9. Entries will be judged during the week of *(insert date)*.

10. All entries become the property of *(insert name of school/district)*.

11. Winners will be determined by a committee of judges.

<u>CONTEST PRIZES:</u>

1. A number of winning poems will be selected from each grade level.

2. The winning poems will be printed into a booklet and *(designate number)* copy(ies) distributed to each class and to the school library.

3. A copy of the booklet of reading-promoting poems will also be awarded to each student whose poem is selected as a winner and included in the booklet.

READING BUMPER-STICKER SLOGAN CONTEST

This is a terrific contest you will want to consider implementing at least once every couple of years. The winning bumper sticker entry is printed as a real bumper sticker and distributed to the winner and to classrooms within the school or school district. Additional bumper stickers can be sold to teachers, parents, and the community as a school money maker, if desired.

BACKGROUND INFORMATION FOR CONTEST COORDINATOR(S)

To get an overview of the contest, read the sample READING BUMPER-STICKER SLOGAN CONTEST announcement flier. Before developing the flier for your contest, call several printing companies to find out the cost of printing bumper stickers. Be sure to inquire about the cost of printing the bumper stickers on vinyl, not on paper. (Bumper stickers printed on paper fade and wash out when rained on and, therefore, cannot be used as real bumper stickers on cars.)

Once you have determined the least expensive place to have the bumper stickers printed and know the printing costs for different quantities of bumper stickers, you are ready to plan your contest. With information on the amount of money available to implement the contest and the printing costs of the bumper stickers, determine how many bumper stickers you can have printed. Then determine how you will distribute the winning bumper sticker. You will need to think through such questions and possibilities as the following:

1. How many bumper stickers will you give to the winner?

2. Will you distribute one to each classroom?

3. Will you give one to each school library in the school district?

4. Will you give one to each teacher in the building to be applied to the bumpers of his or her car?

5. Do you want to have extras printed and sold to parents to raise money to cover the costs of the printing of the bumper stickers for the contest? Selling the bumper stickers to parents, etc., has the added advantage of promoting reading in the community by having the reading-promoting bumper stickers on numerous cars in the community! It can also be a good public relations tool for the school or school district.

As you start generating ideas of how you would like to distribute the winning bumper stickers for maximum exposure, you may become concerned about printing costs and the realities of your contest budget. While selling the bumper stickers to students, parents, etc., can be one way to cover printing expenses, covering the cost in this way is dependent on sales. If they don't sell as easily as expected, you may be stuck.

Another viable alternative to consider is that of contacting a local business and asking its sponsorship of this activity in the form of paying for the printing of the bumper stickers.

If you decide to try to find a local business to provide funding for the contest, be sure you have done your homework in advance. Have the number of bumper stickers you wish to have printed and the total cost of the printing figured. Then, present your contest plans, the costs, and your request for financial support of the activity to the business you have selected to contact. Many local businesses are *very* willing to help schools by supporting worthwhile activities!

If, for some reason, the first company you contact declines to underwrite the cost of the contest, don't be discouraged. Simply contact another local company or business. You will quickly find one willing and eager to support it.

With the cost and quantity of bumper stickers in hand for your contest, you are ready to think through and plan other aspects of your contest.

1. Which grade levels will your contest include?

2. Will the contest be for your school only or will it include other schools within your district?

3. When will you distribute fliers announcing your READING BUMPER-STICK-ER CONTEST?

4. What will be the deadline date for entries to be received?

5. Who will be designated to receive the contest entries?

6. Who will serve as judges for the contest? Possibilities might include your school district superintendent and other administrators and supervisors, prominent individuals within the community, etc. Three or four judges will be needed.

7. Are you going to provide free hamburger or perhaps pizza certificates to a number of "runners up" at each grade level to increase recognition for some of the other great bumper sticker entries? If so, you will need to contact a local fast-food restaurant, explain the contest and its purpose, and ask if the restaurant would be willing to provide free food certificates to help promote reading and their restaurant at the same time.

Once you have the details of your READING BUMPER-STICKER SLOGAN CONTEST thought through and worked out, you are ready to prepare the contest announcement flier. Use the sample contest announcement as a model in developing your flier.

A winning bumper sticker from a Wayne County Schools (Ohio) READING BUMPER STICKER CONTEST.

ANNOUNCING

READING BUMPER-STICKER SLOGAN CONTEST

Students in grades *(insert grade levels)* are invited to enter the *(insert name of school or school district)* READING BUMPER-STICKER CONTEST.

CONTEST RULES:

1. The contestant will submit a slogan on a 3" × 15" piece of white paper.

2. The slogan should emphasize the fun of reading and/or the importance of reading.

3. The contestant's name, grade level, teacher, and school should be written legibly on the back of the bumper sticker entry.

4. All entries should be submitted to *(insert name of staff member to receive entries)* no later than *(insert date)*.

5. Entries will be judged the week of *(insert date)*.

6. All entries become the property of *(insert name of school or school district)* and will not be returned.

7. Winners will be determined by a committee of judges.

CONTEST PRIZES:

1. The bumper sticker judged to be the GRAND WINNER will be printed as a real bumper sticker and will be distributed on a limited basis with each *(classroom or school)* receiving one bumper sticker. Additional copies of the bumper sticker will be available at a cost of *(designate amount)*.

2. The GRAND WINNER will receive five bumper stickers containing his or her winning slogan.

3. Other winners at each grade level will receive certificates for free hamburgers at *(insert name of cooperating local fast food restaurant)*.

SONG LYRICS CONTEST

This reading-promoting contest is designed much like the WRITE-A-READING-POEM CONTEST. It encourages children to think about and write about the pleasure and/or importance of reading and to have fun in the process! Setting up and implementing this contest is easy.

BACKGROUND INFORMATION FOR CONTEST COORDINATOR(S)

Begin by reading the sample flier announcing the SONG LYRICS CONTEST to give you an overview of the contest. Basically, you need to decide the following things:

1. Will this contest involve just your school or will it involve all of the schools in your district?

2. Which grade levels will be invited to participate in the contest?

3. When will you distribute fliers announcing the contest?

4. How much time should there be between distributing fliers announcing the contest and the deadline for contest entries?

5. What will be the actual final deadline date for receiving entries?

6. Who will be designated to receive contest entries?

7. Who will serve as judges for the contest?

8. When will the judging take place?

9. Who will be responsible for printing and reproducing the song lyrics into a booklet?

Once you have thought through each of these questions, you are ready to design a flier advertising your SONG LYRICS CONTEST using the general format found in the sample flier.

Students and teachers will enjoy this contest. The judges will be delightfully astonished by the quality and creativity of the entries. Students will be proud to see their song lyrics printed into a booklet. And, parents will be glowing with pride as they show the booklet containing their child's song lyrics to friends and relatives!

NOTE

Be careful not to set the criteria for "winning" so high that only a very few song lyrics are selected. Keep in mind the real purpose of the contest is to make students feel good about reading *and* their song lyric creations. Therefore, the judges will want to select all of the *good* song lyric entries as winners for inclusion in the booklet!

(Sample SONG LYRICS CONTEST announcement.
Adapt or modify to explain your contest.)

ANNOUNCING

SONG LYRICS CONTEST

Students in grades (*insert grade levels*) are invited to enter the (*insert name of school or school district*) SONG LYRICS CONTEST.

<u>CONTEST RULES</u>:

1. The contestant will write original song lyrics emphasizing in some way the fun of reading and/or the importance of reading. The song lyrics should consist of new words to a familiar song.

2. All entries should be written (or typed) neatly on a sheet of tablet paper, notebook paper, or photocopier paper.

3. The name of the song the lyrics accompany must be written on the entry.

4. The contestant may add illustrations to the entry, if desired. However, entries will be judged on the basis of the reading-promoting song lyrics.

5. Small group developed or class developed reading-promoting song lyrics can be submitted.

6. THE READING-PROMOTING SONG LYRICS SHALL BE THE ORIGINAL WORK OF THE INDIVIDUAL STUDENT OR GROUP SUBMITTING IT.

7. The contestant's name, grade level, teacher, and school should be written legibly on the back of the entry.

8. In the case of a class entry or group entry, the grade level, teacher, and school should be written legibly on the back of the entry.

9. All entries should be submitted to (*designate name of individual and location*) <u>no later than</u> (*insert date—day, month, year*).

10. Entries will be judged during the week of (*designate dates*).

11. Entries become the property of (<u>insert name of school or school district</u>) and will not be returned.

12. Winners will be determined by a committee of judges.

ANNOUNCING

SONG LYRICS CONTEST, continued

<u>CONTEST PRIZES</u>:

1. A number of winning song lyrics will be selected from each grade level.

2. The winning song lyrics will be printed into a booklet and two copies distributed to the school libraries in each of the schools within the school district.

3. A copy of the booklet of reading-promoting song lyrics will also be awarded to each student whose song lyrics is selected as a winner and included in the booklet.

4. A copy of the booklet of reading-promoting song lyrics will be awarded to each class whose class song lyrics or group song lyrics is selected as a winner and included in the booklet.

WRITE-A-READING-CHEER CONTEST

This is a fun and easy contest to implement. It involves students writing cheers about the fun and importance of books and reading. The best cheers are then printed into a booklet and distributed to the students whose cheers are selected, to classrooms, and to the school library. This contest works best for grades 5 and up. Many students at grade levels below fifth grade do not understand cheers well enough to enjoy the contest.

BACKGROUND INFORMATION FOR CONTEST COORDINATOR(S)

To implement this contest, begin by reading the sample WRITE-A-READING-CHEER CONTEST announcement to get an overview of the contest. You will need to determine the following as you plan your WRITE-A-READING-CHEER CONTEST:

1. Will the contest be just for your school or will it include other schools within your school district? If so, which ones?

2. What grade levels will you include in the contest?

3. When do you want to distribute fliers announcing the contest?

4. When will your contest entry deadline be?

5. Who will be designated to receive the reading cheer entries?

6. Who will serve as contest judges?

7. Who will be responsible for creating, printing, and distributing the booklet of reading cheers?

Once these things have been decided, you are ready to implement your contest.

NOTE

Be careful that the judges do not set the criteria for "winning" so high that only a very few reading cheers are selected. Keep in mind the real purpose of the contest is to make students feel good about reading *and* their reading cheers. Therefore, the judges will want to select all of the *good* reading cheer entries as winners for inclusion in the booklet!

ANNOUNCING

WRITE-A-READING-CHEER CONTEST

Students in grades *(designate grade levels)* are invited to enter the *(designate school, schools, or district)* WRITE-A-READING-CHEER CONTEST.

<u>CONTEST RULES</u>:

1. The contestant will write an original cheer emphasizing in some way the fun or reading and/or the importance of reading.

2. All entries should be written (or typed) neatly on a sheet of tablet paper, notebook paper, or photocopier paper.

3. Small group developed or class developed reading-promoting cheers can be submitted.

4. The contestant's name, grade, teacher, and school should be written legibly on the back of the entry.

5. In the case of a class entry or group entry, the grade-level teacher and school should be written legibly on the back of the entry.

6. All entries should be submitted to *(designate person and place entries are to be submitted)* <u>no later than</u> *(designate date)*.

7. Entries will be judged during the week of *(designate date)*.

8. Entries become the property of *(designate school or school district)*.

9. Winners will be determined by a committee of judges.

ANNOUNCING

WRITE-A-READING-CHEER CONTEST, continued

CONTEST PRIZES:

1. A number of winning cheers will be selected from each grade level.

2. The cheers will be printed into a booklet and two copies distributed to *(designate your school library, or if this is a district-wide contest, designate two copies to each elementary and middle/Jr. high school in the district)*.

3. A copy of the booklet of reading-promoting cheers will also be awarded to each student whose cheer is selected as a winner and included in the booklet.

4. A copy of the booklet of reading-promoting cheers will be awarded to each class whose class cheer or group cheer is selected as a winner and included in the booklet.

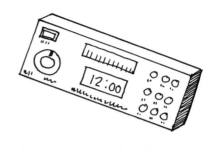

READING RADIO ANNOUNCEMENT CONTEST

This is a great contest that involves students writing approximately 15- to 30-second radio announcements proclaiming in some way the pleasure of books and/or importance of reading. The winning entries are tape recorded and played on a rotating basis on the local radio station. Certificates for free hamburgers at a local restaurant may also be awarded to the winners and runners-up, if desired. This contest encourages students to think about the fun of books and the importance of reading and then to put their thoughts into words.

BACKGROUND INFORMATION FOR CONTEST COORDINATOR(S)

Begin by reading the sample READING RADIO ANNOUNCEMENT CONTEST flier to get a good overview of the contest.

To implement this contest, you will first need to talk to the manager of a local radio station, explain the contest, and ask if the radio station would be willing to broadcast the winning reading radio announcements on a rotating basis over a one- to two-week period. Most radio stations will gladly support a worthwhile activity as a public service.

After the radio station manager has indicated willingness to broadcast the reading radio announcements, you will need to find out how he or she would like the announcements recorded. Can you or some other school personnel tape the individual winners reading their radio announcements or does the radio station want to send someone to record the students reading them?

Next, if you want to add the awarding of free hamburger certificates to the winners and runners-up, you will need to contact a local fast-food restaurant, explain the contest, and ask if they would be willing to contribute free hamburger certificates for contest prizes.

Once these two important contest components are in place, you are ready to proceed with the planning and implementation of your contest. You now must determine the following:

1. Will the contest be just for your school or will it include other schools within your school district? If so, which ones?

2. What grade levels do you want to include in the contest?

3. When do you want to distribute fliers announcing the contest?

4. When will be the contest entry deadline?

5. Who will be designated to receive the reading radio announcement entries?

6. Who will be the contest judges?

7. Who will be responsible for tape recording the winning announcements?

8. Who will be responsible for distributing the free hamburger certificates to the winners and runners up?

When the winning reading radio announcements are being recorded, be sure that someone precedes the recording of each student with something similar to "The following radio announcement, designed to highlight the pleasure and importance of reading, was written and recorded by *(student's name)*, a student in the _____ grade at *(name of school)*." Then comes the student's reading radio announcement.

ANNOUNCING

READING RADIO ANNOUNCEMENT CONTEST

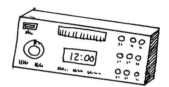

Students in grades (insert grade levels) are invited to enter the *(insert name of school or school district)* RADIO ANNOUNCEMENT CONTEST.

1. Contestants will write 15- to 30-second radio spot announcements emphasizing the fun of reading for pleasure and/or the importance of reading.

2. The contestant's name, grade level, and school should be written legibly on the back of the entry.

3. All entries should be submitted to *(designate name of individual and location)* <u>no later than</u> *(insert time and date—day, month, year).*

4. Entries will be judged on *(insert date).*

5. The winning radio announcements will be tape recorded *(insert date or dates)* and will be played on *(insert name of cooperating radio station)* on a rotating basis throughout the week of *(insert dates).*

6. *(Insert name of individual)* will contact individual winners and will come to their *(indicate school or classroom)* to have the winners record their reading advertisements on tape.

7. Certificates for free hamburgers at *(insert name of cooperating local fast-food restaurant)* will be awarded to the *(insert number)* best radio announcement entries.

Section 7

GETTING THE WHOLE SCHOOL HOOKED ON BOOKS

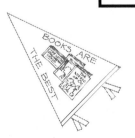

PROMOTING THE LOVE OF BOOKS
AS A WHOLE SCHOOL EFFORT

Promoting children's love of books and reading should be a whole school effort and not just the responsibility of the individual teachers in the building. Teachers definitely need to promote the love of books actively and enthusiastically every day and in many ways in their classrooms. But, it is a shame if schools don't go a step beyond and take further measures to emphasize the joy of reading.

Some schools radiate a love of books and reading that is very noticeable the minute you step into the building. Some schools take every opportunity to encourage children to read for pleasure. Some schools plan whole school activities and events that emphasize the fun of books and reading.

Let's look at some ways a school can radiate a love of books and reading and *make* opportunities to encourage children to get hooked on books.

DECORATE THE WALLS AND HALLS

Decorate those plain walls in the hallways, cafeteria, and library with delightful paintings of scenes and/or characters from popular children's books. The art teacher or high school art students may be willing to help with this project. Some artistically talented parents may also be willing to help with the project. You may also wish to explore the possibility of students in the drafting classes at the high school or vocational school assisting with the artwork.

If these options are not available, pictures of scenes or characters in books can be put in an opaque projector, projected on a wall, and the outline traced onto the walls. The pictures can be painted attractively by volunteers from the PTA or the community in general.

If decorating the walls in the school seems like too formidable a task because of the number of walls, begin with small, manageable painting projects. Gradually, over a period of time, wall by wall the school will become a book character/scene wonderland.

The students, teachers, and school librarian can be involved in helping determine which book character and scenes should be painted on the walls. You may even want to develop a nomination process, including students voting on favorite grade-level selections. If you want to hype the selection process even more, you could allow students to campaign for and make persuasive speeches about the scenes or characters of their choice.

OUR PRINCIPAL READS TO US

The principal can emphasize the pleasure to be found in books by visiting a different class each day to read aloud a super good book to the class. The principal can read a good book to a primary class. For an intermediate class, the principal can read a good short story to the class or can read the next chapter in the book that the teacher has been reading to the class. Whatever the principal chooses to read to the class, he or she should have read it ahead of time and, perhaps, have practiced reading it aloud.

To maximize students' awareness that the principal is actually reading to a different class each day, the room that will be read to on the next day could be selected by a drawing and announced over the PA system with great fanfare. Ham it up!

A SPECIAL SPOT

Setting up a special location in the school where students can go to read a book as a special reward for doing something good can reflect your school's priorities. This special place should be furnished comfortably for relaxing reading. The spe-

cial place could be a pleasant corner in a hallway, a spare classroom, a section of the school library reserved for this purpose, or anywhere spare space can be found.

It is unfortunate that we often make reading a library book seem like punishment. Many times teachers look up and see some students finished with their assigned work and whispering together. We often crossly tell those students to get out a library book and read. The unintended implication is, of course, that the student is misbehaving, therefore, the student should get out a book and read.

We need to give children the definite impression that reading books is a pleasure to be enjoyed, not a punishment to be endured! Having a special location where students can go to read as a reward can help promote the idea that reading is indeed rewarding.

AN EXCLUSIVE SCHOOL-WIDE BOOKWORM CLUB

Your school may want to establish a school-wide Bookworm Club for all children who read more than a certain number of books. Membership in the Bookworm Club should definitely be an honor with special rights and privileges for members only.

Privileges for members might include a special movie once a month shown to members only by the principal in the school library, special school library privileges, and special free reading times.

Begin by establishing a committee of teachers or students and teachers to set up guidelines for the club. The guidelines should include criteria for membership in the club and whether a student stays a member of the club for the entire year once he or she qualifies or whether there will be a criteria for maintaining membership in the club throughout the year.

The committee will need to determine the privileges and benefits for membership. The committee will also need to create a workable system for determining when a student actually qualifies for membership in the Bookworm Club. And, finally, the committee will need to devise a plan for announcing the Bookworm Club and whipping up student interest in becoming a member.

Once the details of the Bookworm Club have been thought through and planned carefully, the Bookworm Club needs to be announced with fanfare.

BUILDING-WIDE SUSTAINED SILENT READING

Sustained silent reading instituted on a building-wide basis truly demonstrates the school's commitment to reading enjoyment and emphasis on encouraging students to develop the reading habit.

When a school institutes sustained silent reading, 15-20 minutes a day is designated when *everyone* in the whole building reads a book or magazine for pleasure. The students read, the teachers read, the principal reads, even the janitors, cooks and any visitors read during this time. Pre-readers "read" by looking at and enjoying picture books.

Sustained silent reading conducted building-wide on a daily basis gets children into a habit of reading for pleasure and gets children into books. Once started, children often find it hard to put down a good book and are eager to get back to reading it at the first opportunity. What an excellent way to hook children on books!

Sustained silent reading also demonstrates to the children that *all* of the adults in the school think reading books is important and really find pleasure in reading.

THE PRINCIPAL READS, TOO

The principal can demonstrate enjoyment of reading by entering a different classroom each day and quietly sitting and reading his or her own book during sustained silent reading time or during other free reading time. Children need to see adults enjoying books. The fact that even the principal takes time to enjoy a book will make a silent statement with a strong impact.

BOOK AND LUNCH CLUB

Establishing a BOOK AND LUNCH CLUB can be a great way to give children more time during the school day to read for pleasure and to convey in yet another way that reading is fun. BOOK AND LUNCH CLUB members enjoy reading books while eating their lunch on designated "meeting" days.

To start a BOOK AND LUNCH CLUB, teachers in your school need to decide which grade-level students will be permitted membership in the club. Next, the frequency of BOOK AND LUNCH CLUB days (days where the members will sit down with books and lunch trays or brown bag lunches and simply enjoy reading their books while munching their lunches) and the room location will need to be determined.

You may want to limit membership to students in grades 3-6 because of their longer attention spans and, therefore, ability to sit and read for longer periods of time. You will also probably limit BOOK AND LUNCH CLUB days to one day a month, or at the most, one day every other week. If BOOK AND LUNCH CLUB days are set too frequently, students will begin to lose interest. In many schools, the school library would be a logical location for the club members to meet to read their books and munch their lunches. However, there may be an even better location in your particular building

Once these specifics have been determined, a Membership Application Form needs to be developed, along with printed Membership Cards. Attractive posters and/or banners advertising the club can be created and hung on walls in the hallways. With enthusiastic teacher fanfare, a special announcement about and explanation of the BOOK AND LUNCH CLUB can be made during an assembly or in the individual classrooms. Students can then be given Membership Application Forms to fill out if they are interested in joining the club. The Membership Application Forms can be turned in to the principal, who then issues official Membership Cards to those students.

Several days before a BOOK AND LUNCH CLUB DAY, posters or banners advertising the BOOK AND LUNCH CLUB DAY should be posted throughout the school. In their classrooms, members should be reminded to have a book to bring to the BOOK AND LUNCH CLUB. Tell them that they will also need to show their Membership Cards to be admitted to the club "meeting."

Shortly before lunchtime begins, the principal, librarian, or a teacher should set up a table and chair outside the library (or other "meeting" location). That person then sits down at the table. As the students arrive with their books and lunch trays, they must show their Membership Cards for admission.

Several teachers with books and lunches of their own should join the group, both to monitor student behavior and to model reading for pleasure while eating.

Students should be allowed to sit at tables or on the floor while reading their books and eating their lunches. This should be a pleasurable and relaxing time for everyone! At the end of the BOOK AND LUNCH CLUB time, students take their lunch trays back to the cafeteria and then return to their classrooms.

BOOK FAIRS

Book fairs have been used by many schools as a way to get more books in the hands of children, to convey to parents the importance of having books in the home, and to provide an inexpensive source of paperback books for children to buy and for parents to buy for their children. In addition, the school's portion of the money from the sale of books at the book fair can be used to purchase books for the school library, sets of paperback books for classroom use, or books to give to students who may not be able to afford to buy books.

If your school does not have a semi-annual book fair, explore the possibility.

LIBRARY ANYTIME

Schools that want to promote reading should have a school library schedule that allows students access to the library to select new books as they need them, as well as on a regularly scheduled basis. Many schools schedule students into the library on a weekly or biweekly basis. The students return books and select new ones at that time only. The student who finishes his or her books before the scheduled library day is out of luck and out of books! This can certainly be a deterrent to developing enthusiastic readers.

When students are allowed to select additional books before school, after school, during lunch periods, or at other times, this problem can be solved easily and children can be kept in books at a rate appropriate for their needs.

LIBRARY TIME FOR PARENTS

Encouraging parents to come to the school library often to select children's books to take home and read aloud to their children is a positive approach to getting parents involved in constructive ways of helping their children become motivated and skilled readers. Children in grades K-6 who are read aloud to *frequently* from wonderful library books develop a range of reading skills at a considerably higher level than children who are not read to as frequently. Beyond that, children who are read to often discover the wonderful stories found in books and become more motivated readers and learners.

While every classroom teacher should definitely be allocating time each day to read aloud to their students, there is a limit to how much time is available for this purpose. To increase the amount of time children are read to each day, we need to involve parents.

Parents need to realize the importance of their reading aloud to their children on a daily basis. And, we need to do everything we can to foster parents' reading aloud to their children.

A very significant way we can encourage parents to read aloud to their children is to provide them with easy access to terrific library books for reading aloud. While the public library is, of course, a source for wonderful books, the fact is some of the parents simply will not go to a public library. Some of those parents, however, would be willing to come to the school to select books from the school library.

With that in mind, your school might want to give serious consideration to having a welcoming policy for parents using the school library to check out children's books. Your school might want to open the school library to parents one afternoon a week, during which time they can come in, browse through the library shelves, and check out children's books. During that time the school librarian could offer to assist parents in the selection of books that are especially good for reading aloud.

EMPHASIZE PARENTS' ROLE IN PROMOTING READING

It is important that a school take an active role in helping parents learn how to nurture the reading habit, reading enthusiasm, and reading skill development of their children. Topics in this area can be made the focal point of PTA meetings, creatively designed parent informational meetings, and send-home newsletters.

The meetings, parent workshops, and/or send-home newsletters should:

1. ENCOURAGE PARENTS TO READ ALOUD TO THEIR CHILDREN AT HOME. Parents need to know the importance of reading aloud to children, grades K-6, on a daily basis. They need to know that it is the NUMBER 1 most effective thing they can do to help their children become better, motivated readers.

2. PROVIDE PARENTS WITH IDEAS OF GOOD BOOKS FOR READING ALOUD. This would be a terrific topic for a PTA meeting. The school librarian, a children's librarian from the local public library, a children's literature professor from a nearby college or university, or someone very knowledgeable in children's books from a local bookstore could be the speaker for the meeting. Showing parents terrific books for reading aloud to their children, telling a little about each of the books, reading aloud from some of the books, and providing parents with a list of good books to read aloud, can be the basis of a highly worthwhile PTA meeting and a highly effective means of getting parents excited about reading aloud.

Newsletters suggesting great books to read aloud, sent home periodically throughout the year, can help maintain parents' commitment to reading aloud. Suggestions of book titles to include in letters can be brainstormed by the teachers in the school. Additional ideas can be drawn from *The New Read-Aloud Handbook* by Jim Trelease.

3. ENCOURAGE PARENTS TO TAKE THEIR CHILDREN TO THE LOCAL PUBLIC LIBRARY ON A FREQUENT BASIS. Perhaps one of the school PTA meetings could actually be held at the local public library to help familiarize parents with the children's section of the library. Some parents who have not been in the public library for many years, if ever, would then be more likely to take their children to the library and more likely to use it themselves.

In addition to or instead of a PTA meeting at the library, school-sponsored tours of the public library aimed specifically at parents could help encourage more parents to use the library and feel at ease at the library.

"BOOKS FOR BABIES" PROGRAM

Your school may want to consider the possibility of trying to reach the parents of newborn children in your community with the message of the importance of reading aloud to children throughout their preschool years. A terrific way to do this is to give each mother of a newborn child a picture book as a "starter" to what will hopefully become the family's collection of read-aloud books. In the front of the book, you could stamp "A gift to your newborn child from _____ Elementary School" (or some similar kind of statement).

Along with the book, an easy-to-read brochure should be provided, explaining the importance of reading aloud to children before they enter kindergarten. It could also list specific school success-oriented advantages that children who have been read to have over children who have not been read to.

Your school might want to apply for a grant, approach a local community-minded business, or other source for funding to cover the cost of purchasing children's picture books to distribute to parents of newborn children.

A well-planned, well-implemented *Books for Babies Program* has the potential of having a tremendous impact on the early literacy development of preschoolers who will be entering your school.

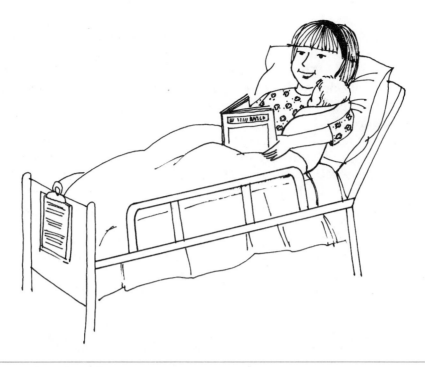

"BOOKS FOR BABES ON BIRTHDAYS" PROGRAM

If you can raise sufficient funding or if the PTA is willing to sponsor the project, you might want to extend the *Books for Babies Program* a step further to a *Books for Babes on Birthdays Program*. This would involve inviting parents to bring their preschoolers to the school on each birthday to receive another book. Of course, preschoolers with birthdays falling on weekends or on holidays and vacations would come to receive their books on a day when school is open.

Extending the program to include *Books for Babes on Birthdays* has a number of very definite benefits for the child and the school: (1) It encourages parents to read to their preschoolers; (2) it assures that all of the participating children in your school's area would have some pleasurable familiarity with books before entering school; (3) the preschoolers get an enjoyable and rewarding introduction into the school setting early on; and (4) it serves as a tool for helping parents of young children have good feelings toward your school and an increased comfort level when contacting the school.

VOLUNTEER READING CORPS

In the vicinity of your school there may be several retired teachers who would enjoy an opportunity to come to your school on a voluntary basis and read to small groups of children. There are probably a number of parents and grandparents who would also be very willing to come in and read to students.

We know that the more children are read to in grades K-6, the higher the level of reading achievement and the higher the level of reading motivation. Therefore, we need to provide as many opportunities as possible for children to hear stories read aloud. All classroom teachers should be reading delightful stories to their students daily. However, teachers are limited in the amount of time they can devote to reading to their students. Their students could benefit from even more exposure to stories being read aloud.

Taking advantage of volunteers who would be willing to read wonderful books to small groups of children can increase opportunities for students to enjoy the many benefits resulting from being read to.

There is always time in the school day when a teacher is working with a small group of students. This is the perfect time for a volunteer to read to another group of students!

A SUMMER READING PROGRAM

Instituting a Summer Reading Program helps keep children reading during the vacation months. A week before school ends, send home a letter explaining the importance of children continuing to read during the summer in order to maintain or improve reading skills, as well as to further establish the reading habit. Explain that the children are being encouraged to read ten or more books during the vacation. All children reading ten or more books will receive a "Bookworm Award" when school resumes in the fall.

Send home a Summer Reading Record Form with the letter to the parents. In the letter explain to the parents that they are to fill in the record sheet each time their child completes a book. On the Summer Reading Record Form the parents should indicate the title of each book the child reads, the date the child finished reading it, and add their initials to each book listed. Explain that the child should return the record sheet to his or her new teacher on the first day of school.

Enthusiastically explain the Summer Reading Program to the students at each grade level and encourage each child to participate.

A week after school begins in the fall, award "Bookworm Awards" to all children who have read the minimum of ten books. The Bookworm Award can be a certificate or whatever the school sets as the award.

The school may wish to give additional special recognition to the students who read the most books at each grade level or to all students reading more than forty books during the summer.

Section 8

SPECIAL BUILDING-WIDE READING-INCENTIVE ACTIVITIES

PEP RALLY FOR BOOKS

How would you like to hear your whole school cheering wildly for books, with high school cheerleaders in their cheerleading outfits leading the cheers? Wouldn't that be exciting? Add to that several of the best-known local high school football players telling your students about some of their favorite books when they were in elementary (or junior high) school. Wouldn't that be even more exciting?

If the whole idea makes you want to stand up and cheer, why don't you organize a pep rally for books for your school? Ask some high school cheerleaders to make up some cheers for books and reading, and then perform the cheers in a pep rally for books and reading at your school. Next, ask two of your school district's best-known high school football players if they would be willing to tell your school's students about some of their favorite books when they were in elementary school (or junior high school). You may also want to have a third football player tell why he thinks reading is so much fun and a fourth football player tell why he believes reading well is important to succeeding in life.

Make arrangements with the high school principal for the selected cheerleaders and football players to come to your school to lead this very special pep rally.

If your school is an elementary school, many of the students may not know what a pep rally is. Therefore, the day before the pep rally, you will want the teachers in your building to enthusiastically tell their students that there will be a pep rally for books at your school. Have them explain that there will be cheerleaders cheering for books and some of the high school football players talking about their favorite books. Then have the teachers talk about what high school pep rallies are like to build the needed background information so that the students will understand what is happening and will excitedly participate in the pep rally for books.

At the designated time, have all the students and teachers gather in the school auditorium. Then, let the pep rally for books begin!

Have the cheerleaders come out on the stage in their cheerleading outfits and shaking their pompoms. Have them perform several cheers. Then have them teach some of the cheers to the students so that the students can shout the cheers with the cheerleaders.

Next, with the cheerleaders moving toward the back of the stage, but still excitedly waving their pompoms, have one of the football players run out on the stage wearing his football uniform, with a football under one arm and a book in his other hand. Have the football player stop center stage, hold up his book, and tell the students the name of the book and briefly tell why it was one of his favorite books when he was in elementary (or junior high) school. Have the second football player come on stage in a similar way and briefly, but enthusiastically, tell about his favorite book.

Next might come another cheer for books led by the cheerleaders, followed by the remaining two football players talking about the fun of books and the importance of reading well to succeed in life. Follow this by another resounding cheer for books. Then end the pep rally by sending the enthusiastic students back to their classrooms to grab a book and READ, READ, READ!

THE PRINCIPAL'S CHALLENGE: CUT OFF MY TIE!

Imagine the delight of students in your school when they get to cut off pieces of the principal's necktie! The students in your school will read like crazy if they think that someone in their classroom will get to cut off a piece of their principal's necktie each time their class reads a certain number of books. Of course, this activity will work best if the principal of the school is a man since a man's necktie is integral to the activity.

To kick off the highly motivating reading-incentive activity, the principal should go to each individual classroom, grades 1-6, and issue a challenge to the students. If the class as a whole reads a total of _____ books, a student in the class will get to cut off a piece of the principal's necktie. And, each time the class as a whole reads another _____ books, someone in the class will get to cut off another chunk of the necktie.

Students will enthusiastically read and read and read! Each morning each teacher can tally the number of books that have been read by his or her class. Whenever the goal is reached by a class, the teacher summons the principal for the tie-cutting ceremony.

When the principal arrives, the class selects a student for the honor of cutting the tie. The student is given a pair of scissors and, to the cheers and applause of classmates, proceeds to cut off a chunk of the principal's necktie. Pieces of the tie "won" over a period of weeks can be tacked on the class bulletin board as trophies.

Of course, each day that the challenge is in effect, the principal should be seen walking around the school wearing a necktie with pieces cut off. Over a period of time it will get shorter and shorter and shorter! Every so often, the principal will have to begin again with a new tie. The students will be eager each day to check out the length of the principal's necktie. They will delight in seeing it get shorter and shorter!

This reading-incentive challenge can be in place for anywhere from two weeks to a month. If it is extended too long, it loses its impact.

THE PRINCIPAL'S CHALLENGE: MAKE ME WALK!

Students in your school will delight in the prospect of making the principal walk to school—especially if the principal lives some distance from the school. They will read with added enthusiasm if the number of books read in one week by the student body is tied in with the principal *having* to walk to school.

To get this activity going, on a Friday the principal announces to students (grades 1-6) that if, as a whole, the students in the school read a total of _____ books by the following Friday, he or she will walk to school on (specify a day the following week). The principal can really ham it up in issuing the challenge, "Make me walk, if you can!"

Each morning of the next week the number of books read by the students in each class can be totaled. Then, with official fanfare, the number of books read by all of the classes is added up and added on to the number from the preceding day(s). The grand total is posted daily on a large chart.

When the school reaches the challenge number of books read, the number is proclaimed and the students and their teachers celebrate and congratulate themselves for contributing to the successful reaching of the school goal. Now the students and teachers begin a countdown to the day their principal *must* walk to school.

On the designated day, rain or shine, the principal begins his or her walk to school, timing arrival at school about fifteen minutes after school begins. About five minutes before the principal's expected arrival time, the students and teachers gather on the school grounds to wait for the principal's arrival. Students and teachers wait with eager anticipation. As the principal comes into view, excited clapping begins. As the principal arrives at the schoolyard—huffing and puffing (hamming it up!)—the students begin to cheer. The students will love it.

The local newspaper or television station will love it, too. Have reporters and photographers on hand so that it can become the basis of a terrific newspaper report with pictures and all. Or, better yet, it could be featured on the evening news on television!

VARIATION

If the principal lives too far away, too close by, or would have to walk along a dangerous highway, think of another consequence for the principal—one that would delight the students and make them want to read, read, read. The teachers and principal can brainstorm ideas together, then select an appropriate one.

CLASSROOM DOORS PROCLAIM FAVORITE BOOKS

Imagine the interest in books proclaimed by a school in which every classroom door is decorated to represent the favorite children's book of the students in that classroom. And, imagine the fun the students in each class have deciding which book to show on their door. Add to that the oohs and ahs as the students walk the hallways of the school looking at the decorated doors. This is certainly a whole-school reading-motivation activity your school will want to implement!

To implement this school-wide activity, the teachers and the principal need to select a week in which all classes will be involved in planning and decorating classroom doors to depict favorite children's books. A deadline day for the completion of all door decorations should also be established. During planning stages, determine how long the classroom door decorations should stay in place. You might consider a month from the start of the door decorations to the dismantling.

Next, teachers should enthusiastically tell their students about the school-wide door decorating. Together, the teacher and students in each class select the book they wish to depict on their classroom door. After each classroom has selected the book they want, the door decorating begins. In most cases, the first step will be covering the outside of the classroom door with colored bulletin board paper. Then the real fun begins!

In the primary grades, teachers may have to become greatly involved with creating the door decorations. However, at the intermediate and junior high school level, students and teachers can work together to create the door decorations.

The originality of students and teachers in designing and creating the door decorations is exciting and the results will be amazing.

HIGH SCHOOL ATHLETES TALK BOOKS

Elementary school students look up to high school students who "star" on the football and basketball teams. So take advantage of that. Let's have those athletes also be "reading role models" for our students.

To do this, ask high school star football and basketball players to volunteer to visit fourth, fifth, and sixth grade classes to give enthusiastic "sales pitches" on books they read and enjoyed when they were in the intermediate grades. Ask the athletes to wear their team uniforms and carry footballs or basketballs. Ask them also to bring along copies of the books they are going to talk about. That way, as they are talking about a book, they can hold it up for everyone to see. Have the high school athletes visit the classes in groups of two or three, each group telling the children about several books they especially enjoyed. Ask them to really "talk up" books!

The intermediate grade level children will enjoy seeing and listening to the football and basketball players. And, the children will eagerly beg for turns to read the books presented by the high school athletes.

Children in first, second, and third grades will also respond with eager and rapt attention to the high school athletes. Ask some of the athletes to read aloud to the various primary-level classes from good books that the teachers have selected. Be sure to give the high school athletes an opportunity to read the books to themselves in advance of their visit to the classes. That way they can be familiar with the stories they will be reading aloud.

SCHOOL CAFETERIA LUNCH MENU À LA BOOKS!

Immerse the students in your school in books in yet another way. For one week, one week of each month or for one month have the names of the items on the school lunch menu renamed in terms of specific books, a different book for each day's menu.

For example, Monday's lunch menu might be:

Peter Pan Day Menu:

Captain Hook's Favorite	(fish sandwich)
Fried Tinkerbell Taters	(French fries)
Alligator Pears	(pears with green food coloring)
Peter Pan Cookies	(peanut butter cookies)
Magic Milk	(chocolate milk)

Teachers and cafeteria staff can work together to come up with creative menus based on books. Their creativity will be amazing and the students in school will love it!

NAME AND DECORATE SCHOOL HALLWAYS FOR BOOKS

Let your school's enthusiasm about books and reading be obvious from the moment someone sets foot in your building. Let your school's enthusiasm about books and reading be internalized by each and every one of the students and teachers in the school.

Name each of the hallways in your school with names related to books. Then decorate each hallway to reflect the book the hallway name represents. For example, one hallway might be named "YELLOW BRICK ROAD." The hallway could then have a trail of yellow bricks, made out of yellow construction paper, along one of the walls of the hall. In addition, a picture of Dorothy (enlarged and drawn on bulletin board paper) could be cut out and attached to the wall. Other hallways could be named and decorated to represent other books or other parts of the same book.

Staff members can brainstorm ideas together to come up with hall names and decoration ideas. Or, they might wish to come up with a list of possibilities and let students vote to determine which ones will be used.

Once the hallways are named and decorated, you will be able to feel students' excitement and pleasure abound. The halls literally proclaim the pleasure of books.

The hall names and decorations might be left in place for one or two months, then removed. The halls can be renamed and decorated to reflect favorite books each year. In this way, it becomes new and exciting each year.

While the halls are decorated, be sure to invite a reporter from the local newspaper to get photos and an article for the newspaper. Let the public know about the good things your school is doing!

FAVORITE BOOK DISPLAY

It is time to clear the trophies and/or other items out of the hall display case, at least for a few weeks, and put in a truly student interest-grabbing book display. This book display, however, has a very special twist. It is a display of the favorite children's books of each of the school's teachers and the principal. In front of each book in the display is placed a card indicating the name of the individual whose favorite book it is.

The students will be fascinated. Stand back and watch students begin avidly reading the favorite children's books of some of the very important people in their lives.

To create this display, each teacher and the principal writes down the name of his or her favorite book when he or she was a child. These books are then collected and placed in the display case with name cards in front of the displayed books to indicate whose favorite book each is. The name cards can be made from

3" × 5" unlined file cards folded lengthwise so that they stand up easily. (NOTE: Be sure the teachers and principal select books that are still in print and available.)

Now add the caption OUR FAVORITE BOOKS WHEN WE WERE CHILDREN to the display and watch the students flock to the display case. The students will look again and again at this display! Their curiosity and interest will be boundless—and the message it sends is loud and clear.

USED-BOOK DONATIONS TO CLASSROOM LIBRARIES

The more students read, the better their reading skills. In addition, the more wonderful books they read, the more they will love to read. Given these facts, students need to have terrific books readily accessible for their reading pleasure.

A good school library filled with delightful books is a great start. But, the school library that students visit once or twice a week is simply not enough. Classrooms need to have bookshelves loaded with inviting books that constantly lure students to read for pleasure. Frequently, however, the number of trade books found in classrooms is severely limited. And, school budget restraints usually make it unlikely that much can be done to increase significantly the number of trade books in individual classrooms.

If the number of trade books in the individual classroom libraries in your school is of a limited nature, you may want to consider soliciting good children's books from an untapped resource within your community—the *community*. An article in the school newsletter to parents asking for donations of children's books that are still in good condition but that have been outgrown by their children, can result in a bonanza of books to add to classroom libraries. An article in the local newspaper explaining the need for and requesting donations of used children's books can expand the base of book donations even wider.

As boxes upon boxes of donated children's books begin arriving at your school, it will be necessary to sort through them to ensure appropriateness of the books, to weed out ones that are damaged or "too well used," and to make sure that inappropriate markings or words have not been added to some of the pages. Finally, it will need to be determined which books will go to which classrooms.

A committee consisting of the school librarian, several teachers, and several volunteer parents might be established to sort through the books, do the "quality control check," and distribute the books to classrooms. This might even be taken on as a PTA/PTO project. If the PTA/PTO does choose to make this their project, it will be important to have a librarian familiar with children's books and some teachers involved with the sorting and distribution. Teachers and librarians who are familiar with children's books will help insure that only suitable books reach classroom shelves and the books are placed at appropriate grade levels.

The results will be well worth the effort! Soon all of the bookcases in the classrooms in your school will be brimming with wonderful books to excite students and lure them to read, read, read.

BEST BOOK BALLOON LAUNCH

A Best Book Balloon Launch enhances excitement about books. Give each child a balloon and a piece of paper, approximately 2 inches by 4 inches in size. Have each child write a note on the paper stating the name of the best book he or she has read this year, his or her name and school address, and a request that whoever finds the balloon send back a postcard or a letter indicating where the balloon was found. Next, laminate the notes. As you cut the notes out of the laminating film, be sure that you round off the corners so the stiff, sharp corners of laminating film won't end up puncturing the balloons. Now, using a paper punch, punch a hole in each note.

Next, each child is given a helium-filled balloon, tied tightly and with a 15-20 inch piece of string securely attached. The children now tie their notes to the strings of their balloons. (Have the students do this inside the school, preferably in a room with a fairly low ceiling. In this way, if a student accidentally lets go of the string while tying on the note, the balloon will only float up to the ceiling and can be retrieved. If a balloon gets away from a child outside, it is gone!) Younger children may need assistance in tying the note onto the balloon string.

When all of the children have their balloons ready for launching, it is time for everyone to head out to the schoolyard for the launch. When everyone has gathered in the schoolyard, it is time to announce, with great fanfare, the beginning of the countdown to balloon launch! Ten . . . nine . . . eight . . . seven . . . six . . . five . . . four . . . three . . . two . . . one . . . balloons away! Watching the balloons soar up into the sky and away out of sight is a thrill in itself for the children.

On a windy day the balloons will really travel, sometimes across several states. Students will be very excited as they start receiving letters and postcards from finders of their balloons. A large map of the United States can be set up in the school library. Each time a letter comes back to a student, the student can stick a pin in the map indicating the location where his or her balloon was found. Some of the best letters and postcards can be read to the whole school over the school PA system.

TEACHERS DISGUISED AS BOOK CHARACTERS

The students in your school will be delighted to see the teachers in the building dressed as book characters. Their thoughts will focus on books as they try to identify which characters the teachers are dressed to represent. Begin by setting a day when all of the teachers come to school dressed as book characters. The principal, librarian, secretary, cafeteria staff, and custodians may also wish to participate in the fun by dressing as book characters.

Students can have a contest trying to identify the characters the teachers are dressed to represent. Each child can be given a contest entry form with the teachers' and other participating staff members' names listed vertically along the left side of the page. The students look over the costumes of the teachers. Beside each staff member's name on the contest entry form, students write the name of the book character they think that individual is dressed to represent.

During the day the teachers and other participating staff members refrain from telling the students the names of the characters they represent. Even if the students beg for hints, the book characters keep their identities a secret. As they figure out the characters' identities, the students should keep their answers to themselves, writing them secretly on their contest entry forms only.

An hour before school is over all contest entry forms can be collected for judging. The students who have correctly identified all of the characters are declared winners. The contest winners can be announced the next morning. This will allow time for the judges to look over all of the entry forms and determine winners.

After the contest entry forms have been collected, an assembly can be held. Each staff member can step out on the stage and identify the book character he or she is dressed to represent. Clowning around and hamming it up on the part of the book characters is very much in order!

BOOK CHARACTER DRESS-UP DAY

Having a Book Character Dress-Up Day accentuates the fun of books. On this designated day everyone in the school comes to school dressed as a favorite story character. Students, teachers, cafeteria staff, custodians, and the principal all dress up on this day!

A book character parade can be held. Judging can determine the prize-winning costume at each grade level. And, contests can be held in individual classrooms as children try to guess who is dressed as what character.

The fun of books truly radiates from a school on Book Character Dress-Up Day!

BOOK SKIT DAY

Having a Book Skit Day is another way of letting children further enjoy books they have read and share their enjoyment of those books with other children. Begin by designating a specific date as Book Skit Day. Each class then selects a book about which it would like to present a short skit. A week before Book Skit Day each class is busy planning, preparing, and practicing its skit with the help of the teacher. The skit should be approximately five minutes long and can be an event from a book or, if the story is short, an enactment of the entire story. Props, scenery, and costumes can be planned and prepared.

The key to a successful Book Skit Day is really limiting the skits to about five minutes. If the skits drag out too long, students watching the skits will get bored and their pleasure in watching the skits will be lost.

On Book Skit Day an assembly can be held so that each class can present its skit.

In buildings with large numbers of classes, a manageable number of classes can be chosen to give their skits for the school one afternoon. Another group of classes can prepare and present skits another time.

BOOK SWAP DAYS

Having a school-wide book swap two or three times a year helps keep lots of "new" books in the hands of the children in your school. You might call this a terrific recycling project!

Let the children in your school bring from home any books they have read and would like to trade for other books. Be sure the children understand that they can only bring children's books and the books must be in decent shape. All books are taken to a designated location. Each student is give a ticket for each book he or she brings in for trading: one color ticket for each paperback book, another color ticket for each hardcover book. The school may also want to buy some additional children's books at garage sales to add to the book swap. This will help ensure that on the book swap day there are enough books to select from so that all children can find books they wish to have. The children should bring in their books for swapping the week preceding the Book Swap Day.

When the actual Book Swap Day arrives, all of the books are laid out on tables with the paperback books separated from the hardcover books. You may also wish to separate books according to primary-level and intermediate-level.

Students with tickets select paperback books equal to the number of paperback book tickets they have and hardcover books equal to the number of hardcover book tickets. When the students have selected their books, they "pay" for them by turning in their book tickets to the ticket-taker. Only students who have brought in books for the book swap can select books.

A book swap, without a doubt, is an excellent method of recycling books and getting more books into the hands of developing bookworms.

STUDENT-CREATED READING POSTERS

Conducting a school Reading Poster Contest can give students in the school an opportunity to creatively think about and express their appreciation of books and reading. Give each child, grades 1-6, a 12" × 18" or 18" × 24" sheet of white drawing paper. Let each child design a poster that emphasizes the pleasure of reading or the importance of reading. Posters can be colored with crayons, colored pencils, or felt-tip markers or can be painted with tempera paints or watercolors.

One or more winning posters can be selected from each grade level. The winning posters can be displayed in the school library with a construction-paper blue ribbon attached to each one.

Other well-done posters can be called Runners-Up. The runner-up posters can be displayed around the school, at the local public library, in the windows of nearby stores, community centers, and/or nursing homes.

Section 9

READING-MOTIVATION BULLETIN BOARDS

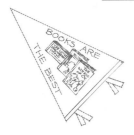

BOOKS ARE DOGGONE GOOD!

MATERIALS

> white bulletin board paper
> permanent felt-tip markers (assorted colors)
> scissors
> stapler
> opaque projector (or overhead projector and transparency)

PREPARATION

Cover bulletin board with white bulletin board paper. Use an opaque projector to project the "Books Are Doggone Good" bulletin board pattern onto the white paper. Trace the lettering and picture onto the bulletin board with a black felt-tip marker. Then color in the picture with the other markers.

NOTE

If an opaque projector is not available, make a transparency of the bulletin board pattern. Then, using an overhead projector, project the illustration onto the bulletin board paper and trace.

BOOKS ARE DOGGONE GOOD!

BOOKS ARE LIKE CANDY BARS . . .
YOU ENJOY THEM FROM BEGINNING TO END

MATERIALS

> white or yellow bulletin board paper
> permanent felt-tip markers (assorted colors)
> scissors
> stapler
> opaque projector (or overhead projector and transparency)

PREPARATION

Cover the bulletin board with the bulletin board paper. Use an opaque projector to project the "Books Are Like Candy Bars..." bulletin board pattern onto the white or yellow paper. Trace the lettering and picture onto the bulletin board paper with a black felt-tip marker. Then color in the picture and lettering with the other markers.

OPTIONAL

Instead of using the illustration of candy bars provided for the bulletin board, you may wish to use real candy bar wrappers. Ask the students to bring in wrappers from some of their favorite candy bars. Staple them, tape them, or glue them to the bulletin board in place of the illustration to form an eye-catching display to go with the caption.

NOTE

If an opaque projector is not available, make a transparency of the bulletin board pattern. Then, using an overhead projector, project the illustration onto the bulletin board paper and trace.

Books are like Candy Bars

you enjoy them from Beginning to End

IMPROVE YOUR IMAGE . . . BE SEEN WITH A BOOK

MATERIALS

> colored bulletin board paper
> permanent felt-tip markers (assorted colors)
> crayons
> stapler
> opaque projector (or overhead projector and transparency)

PREPARATION

Cover a bulletin board with bulletin board paper. Use an opaque projector to project the "Improve Your Image..." pattern onto the colored paper. Trace the caption lettering and picture onto the bulletin board paper with various appropriate colors of felt-tip markers. Then, using colored felt-tip markers and crayons, color in the picture. This quick and easy reading motivating bulletin board is now complete.

NOTE

If an opaque projector is not available, make a transparency of the bulletin board pattern. Then, using an overhead projector, project the illustration onto the bulletin board paper for tracing.

IMPROVE YOUR IMAGE

BE SEEN WITH A BOOK

146

GET WRAPPED UP IN A GOOD BOOK

MATERIALS

    light blue bulletin board paper
    white bulletin board paper
    black permanent felt-tip marker
    scissors
    stapler
    tape or masking tape
    book covers (optional)
    opaque projector (or overhead projector and transparency)

PREPARATION

Cover a bulletin board with light blue bulletin board paper. Use an opaque projector to project the caption lettering onto the bulletin board. Trace the lettering onto the bulletin board with a permanent black felt-tip marker.

Tape a sheet of white bulletin board paper to a chalkboard. (You may wish to tape several sheets of newspaper behind the bulletin board paper to absorb any felt-tip marker ink that might soak through the bulletin board paper.) Next, using an opaque projector, project the mummy onto the white paper. Using the black felt-tip pen, trace the mummy onto the paper. Cut out the mummy and staple it onto the bulletin board.

NOTE

If an opaque projector is not available, make a transparency of the bulletin board pattern. Then, using an overhead projector, project the illustration onto the bulletin board paper to trace.

GET WRAPPED UP

IN A GOOD BOOK

NOTHING BEATS A GOOD BOOK!

MATERIALS

> white bulletin board paper
> permanent felt-tip markers (assorted colors)
> scissors
> stapler
> cut-out letters (optional)
> opaque projector (or overhead projector and transparency)

PREPARATION

Cover a bulletin board with white bulletin board paper. Use an opaque projector to project the bulletin board pattern onto the white paper. Then trace the picture onto the bulletin board paper using a felt-tip black marker and color it with appropriate colors of markers. Staple cut-out letters or trace the lettering from the caption to complete the bulletin board.

NOTE

If an opaque projector is not available, make a transparency of the bulletin board pattern. Then, using an overhead projector, project the illustration onto the bulletin board paper to trace.

NOTHING BEATS A GOOD BOOK!

TIME OUT FOR A GOOD BOOK

MATERIALS

light blue bulletin board paper
white bulletin board paper
permanent felt-tip markers
scissors
stapler
opaque projector (or overhead projector and transparency)

PREPARATION

Cover a bulletin board with light blue bulletin board paper. Use an opaque projector to project the caption lettering onto the bulletin board. Trace the lettering onto the bulletin board with a black felt-tip marker. Trace and color the bushes in the background of the illustration with a green felt-tip marker.

Tape a sheet of white bulletin board paper to a chalkboard. (You may wish to tape several sheets of newspaper behind the bulletin board paper to absorb any felt-tip marker ink that might soak through the bulletin board paper.) Next, using an opaque projector, project the bulletin board picture onto the white paper, trace the picture with a black felt-tip marker, and color in the picture with markers. Cut out the pilgrim, log and gun, and the turkey. Staple them onto the bulletin board.

NOTE

If an opaque projector is not available, make a transparency of the bulletin board pattern. Then, using an overhead projector, project the illustration onto the bulletin board paper to trace.

TIME OUT FOR A GOOD BOOK

TIME TO RELAX WITH A GOOD BOOK!

MATERIALS

white bulletin board paper
permanent felt-tip markers (assorted colors)
crayons
stapler
cut-out letters (optional)
opaque projector (or overhead projection and transparency)

PREPARATION

Cover the bulletin board with white bulletin board paper. Use an opaque projector to project the "Time to Relax With a Good Book" pattern onto the bulletin board. Trace the picture onto the bulletin board paper using a felt-tip black marker. Then color the picture with appropriate colors of felt-tip markers or crayons. Staple cut-out letters or trace the lettering to form the caption to complete the bulletin board.

NOTE

If an opaque projector is not available, make a transparency of the bulletin board pattern. Then, using an overhead projector, project the illustration onto the bulletin board paper to trace.

BOOKS ARE SO PURR-FECT!

MATERIALS

light blue bulletin board paper
white bulletin board paper
permanent felt-tip markers (assorted colors)
colored pencils (assorted colors)
scissors
stapler
opaque projector (or overhead projector and transparency)

PREPARATION

Cover a bulletin board with light blue bulletin board paper. Use an opaque projector to project the caption lettering onto the bulletin board. Trace the lettering onto the bulletin board with a felt-tip marker.

Tape a large sheet of white bulletin board paper to a chalkboard. (You may wish to tape several sheets of newspaper behind the bulletin board paper to absorb any felt-tip marker ink that might soak through the bulletin board paper.) Next, using an opaque projector, project the bulletin board picture onto the white paper. Trace the picture with a black felt-tip marker. Then color in the picture with markers and colored pencils. Cut out the cat, pillow and book, and the other books. Staple them onto the bulletin board.

NOTE

If an opaque projector is not available, make a transparency of the bulletin board pattern. Then, using an overhead projector, project the illustration onto the bulletin board paper to trace.

BOOKS ARE SO PURR-FECT!

DON'T GET LEFT OUT IN THE COLD—READ

MATERIALS

white bulletin board paper
permanent felt-tip markers (assorted colors)
colored pencils (assorted colors)
scissors
stapler
opaque projector (or overhead projector and transparency)

PREPARATION

Cover the bulletin board with white bulletin board paper. Use an opaque projector to project the lettering and pattern onto the white paper. Trace the picture and lettering onto the bulletin board with a black felt-tip marker. Then color in the letters and picture with appropriate colors of markers and colored pencils. You may wish to color the opening in the igloo yellow with some shading of orange to convey warmth inside the igloo.

NOTE

If an opaque projector is not available, make a transparency of the bulletin board pattern. Then, using an overhead projector, project the illustration onto the bulletin board paper to trace.

DON'T GET LEFT OUT IN THE COLD

READING IS LIKE FINDING A POT OF GOLD

MATERIALS

light green bulletin board paper
white bulletin board paper
permanent felt-tip markers (assorted colors)
colored pencils (assorted colors)
scissors
stapler
scotch tape or masking tape
opaque projector (or overhead projector and transparency)

PREPARATION

Cover a bulletin board with light green bulletin board paper. Use an opaque projector to project the caption lettering onto the bulletin board. Trace the lettering onto the bulletin board with a felt-tip marker.

Tape a large sheet of white bulletin board paper to a chalkboard. (You may wish to tape a couple sheets of newspaper behind the bulletin board paper to absorb any felt-tip marker ink that might soak through the bulletin board paper.) Next, using an opaque projector, project the bulletin board picture onto the white paper. Trace the picture with a black felt-tip marker. Then color the picture with markers and colored pencils. Cut out the leprechaun on the pot of gold and staple it onto the bulletin board. Cut out the books and the gold coins and staple them onto the bulletin board.

NOTE

If an opaque projector is not available, make a transparency of the bulletin board pattern. Then, using an overhead projector, project the illustration onto the bulletin board paper to trace.

Reading is like finding

A POT of GOLD

READING IS LIKE JOGGING . . .
IT EXERCISES YOUR MIND

MATERIALS

white bulletin board paper
permanent felt-tip markers (assorted colors)
crayons
stapler
opaque projector (or overhead projector and transparency)

PREPARATION

Cover a bulletin board with white bulletin board paper. Use an opaque projector to project the "Reading Is Like Jogging..." pattern onto the bulletin board. Trace the title lettering and the picture onto the bulletin board paper with various appropriate colors of felt-tip markers. Color in the jogger's hair and clothing with various colors of crayon. This quick and easy bulletin board is now complete.

NOTE

If an opaque projector is not available, make a transparency of the bulletin board pattern. Then, using an overhead projector, project the illustration onto the bulletin board paper to trace.

READING IS LIKE JOGGING...

IT EXERCISES YOUR MIND

162

I GO "QUACKY" OVER BOOKS

MATERIALS

light blue bulletin board paper
yellow bulletin board paper
orange construction paper
permanent felt-tip markers (assorted colors)
old newspaper (optional)
scissors
stapler
tape or masking tape
opaque projector (or overhead projector and transparency)

PREPARATION

Cover a bulletin board with light blue bulletin board paper. Use an opaque projector to project the pattern onto the bulletin board. Trace the lettering and the picture, except the ducks, onto the bulletin board paper with various appropriate colors of felt-tip markers.

Tape a fairly large sheet of yellow bulletin board paper to a chalkboard. (You may wish to tape several sheets of newspaper behind the bulletin board paper to absorb any felt-tip marker ink that might soak through the bulletin board paper.) Next, using an opaque projector, project the picture of the ducks onto the yellow paper. Trace each of the three ducks, minus the bills, with a felt-tip marker. Remove the yellow bulletin board paper from the chalkboard and set aside. Tape pieces of orange construction paper to the chalkboard and trace each of the duck bills with a black felt-tip marker. Next, cut out the three ducks and the bills.

Staple the ducks onto the pond on the bulletin board. Then staple the bills onto the ducks. Your bulletin board is now complete.

NOTE

If an opaque projector is not available, make a transparency of the bulletin board pattern. Then, using an overhead projector, project the illustration onto the bulletin board paper to trace.

I GO "QUACKY" OVER BOOKS!

164

CAMP OUT UNDER THE STARS WITH A GOOD BOOK

MATERIALS

light blue bulletin board paper
white bulletin board paper
permanent felt-tip markers (assorted colors)
colored pencils (assorted colors)
scissors
stapler
tape or masking tape
opaque projector (or overhead projector and transparency)

PREPARATION

Cover the bulletin board with light blue bulletin board paper. Use an opaque projector to project the caption lettering onto the bulletin board. Trace the lettering onto the bulletin board with a felt-tip marker.

Tape a large sheet of white bulletin board paper to a chalkboard. (You may wish to tape several sheets of newspaper behind the bulletin board paper to absorb any felt-tip marker ink that might soak through the bulletin board paper.) Next, using an opaque projector, project the bulletin board picture onto the white paper. Trace the picture with a permanent black felt-tip marker. Then, color the picture with markers and colored pencils. Cut out the picture, including the individual stars, and staple them onto the bulletin board.

NOTE

If an opaque projector is not available, make a transparency of the bulletin board pattern. Then, using an overhead projector, project the illustration onto the bulletin board paper to trace.

CAMP OUT UNDER THE STARS

WITH A GOOD BOOK

GOING ON A TRIP? . . . TAKE SOME BOOKS WITH YOU

MATERIALS

white bulletin board paper
permanent felt-tip markers (assorted colors)
colored pencils (assorted colors)
scissors
stapler
opaque projector (or overhead projector and transparency)

PREPARATION

Cover a bulletin board with white bulletin board paper. Use an opaque projector to project the "Going on a Trip?..." pattern onto the white paper. Trace the lettering and the picture onto the bulletin board with a permanent black felt-tip marker. Then color the picture with the markers and colored pencils.

NOTE

If an opaque projector is not available, make a transparency of the bulletin board pattern. Then, using an overhead projector, project the illustration onto the bulletin board paper to trace.

GOING ON A TRIP?

TAKE SOME BOOKS WITH YOU

Section 10

BOOKMARKS
AND
BADGES

COLOR, CUT, AND USE BOOKMARKS

Throughout the year give your students delightful reading-promoting bookmarks. Twelve bookmarks are found on the next six pages. Periodically, perhaps once every 4-6 weeks, select one or two of the bookmarks to reproduce and distribute to your students.

Begin by photocopying all six pages of bookmarks. Select the one or two you want to distribute first. Use the photocopies of the selected bookmarks as "originals" for the photocopier. Photocopy the bookmark(s) onto white coverstock or tagboard and distribute one bookmark to each student. Have students color their bookmarks with colored pencils and then cut them out. Students should then write their names on the back of their bookmarks. To make the bookmarks more durable, you may wish to laminate them. The bookmarks are then ready for avid reader use.

TREAT YOURSELF

TO A
GOOD BOOK

SAIL AWAY

WITH A
GOOD BOOK

Read A Book

IT'S A GREAT *CATCH!*

READ- IT READ- IT

DON'T HORSE AROUND

READ A BOOK

READING MAKES ME JUMP FOR JOY!

On a Rainy
Day

Let a book make
it
Shine!

I'd Give Up
A Hundred
Carrots to
Read A Book

READING BADGES

Photocopy any or all of the following reading-promoting badge design circles. Give a badge design circle to each student to color and cut out. Snap each student's badge design circle into a real pin-backed badge using a badge-making kit*. Then, let the students wear with enthusiasm their reading-promoting badges.

* Badge-making equipment and parts can be purchased from:

Badge-A-Minit
348 North 30th Road
Box 800
LaSalle, IL 61301
Phone: 1-800-223-4103

BOOKS ARE #1

Take me to your Books

READING FEVER CATCH IT!

HUG A BOOK!

BE WISE READ!

Think Books!

Section 11

POSTERS TO PROMOTE READING

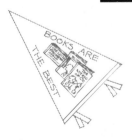

Manufacturers do it. McDonald's does it. Why don't we in education? When businesses want to sell their product, they advertise, advertise, advertise! As educators, we need to wake up. We need to be actively promoting those things we want students to "buy" into.

So, let's get started advertising books! On the next fifteen pages you will find terrific reading-promoting poster ideas for you to reproduce on colored posterboard or railroad board.

Simply select a reading poster you wish to reproduce. Use an opaque projector to project it onto a piece of posterboard. Then, trace the lettering and the illustration onto the posterboard. Next, use colored permanent markers to trace the outline of the illustration and to outline and color in the letters of the caption. Now you are ready to color the illustration with colored pencils or permanent markers. When your poster is complete, be sure to laminate it so that it can be used year after year.

Throughout the year, have reading-promoting posters hanging in your classroom. Be sure to take down old ones and put up new ones periodically. You may also wish to have reading-promoting posters displayed in the hallways throughout the school, in the cafeteria, in the rest rooms, etc. **Put the power of advertising to work for you!**

NOTE

If you do not have an opaque projector to use in reproducing the poster, use the school photocopy machine to make a transparency of the poster in the book. Then, put the transparency on an overhead projector and trace the projected lettering and illustration onto the posterboard.

READING IS

THE CAT'S *Meow*

READING IS A WHALE OF A LOT OF FUN!

BOOKS ARE REAL TAIL-WAGGERS

189

PIG OUT ON A GREAT BOOK

IT PAYS

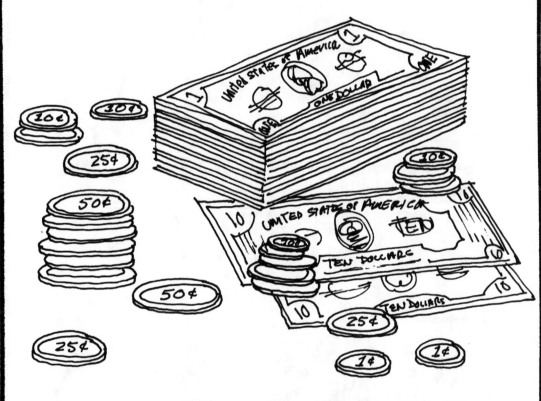

TO READ

TUNE INTO A GOOD BOOK

Reading Is

A KICK!

STAMP OUT BOREDOM

READ

Section 12

READING
CLIP-ART

INDIVIDUAL CLIP-ART PICTURES

These individual clip-art pictures can be either enlarged or reduced on a photocopier to the needed size; cut and taped onto worksheets, teacher-created reading awards, or letters to parents; and then photocopied in needed quantities. Clip-art pictures can also be taped onto transparency originals and used to create terrific transparencies.

Clip-art pictures can also be used as the basis for a reading-motivating bulletin board. Simply place a photocopy of the desired picture in an opaque projector and project the picture onto a bulletin board covered with attractive bulletin board paper. Trace the picture onto the bulletin board paper with markers. Use crayons to color the picture in an eye-catching manner. Then add an appropriate caption. The possibilities are unlimited!

202

204

205

Section 13

STORY-EXTENSION ACTIVITIES

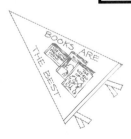

The 12 story-extension activities in this section provide students with another opportunity to think more deeply about and respond to a story they have just completed reading. The activities are primarily writing activities designed to develop students' reading comprehension skills, writing skills, and creative-thinking skills.

These high-interest story-extension activities can be used with most fiction books your students will be reading. They can also be used following many of the stories in the basal reader program in place of the isolated skill/drill worksheets that usually follow basal-reader stories.

MY CRYSTAL BALL SAYS . . .

Title of Story _____   Author _____

    Select two characters from the story. Explain in detail what you think each will be doing in twenty years and tell why. Write your prediction on another sheet of paper. Then attach this page to it.

      Character #1   Character #2

_____   _____

NAME _____

SANTA IS MAKING HIS LIST

Title of Story _____ Author _____

Select a character from the story. Imagine what that character would most like for Christmas and tell why.

Write your explanation on notebook paper. When you have finished, staple this page to your story to make a cover. Then color the Santa picture.

Name of story character:

_____

What that character would most like for Christmas:

_____

THE LEPRECHAUN'S LUCKY
FOUR-LEAF CLOVER

Title of Story _____ Author _____

    Imagine that one of the characters in the story you just read has found a leprechaun's lucky four-leaf clover. That four-leaf clover brings <u>much</u> good luck to the person who has it! Write a story about what happens to that character now that he/she has that fantastic four-leaf clover.

    Write your story on notebook paper. When you have finished, staple this page to your story to make a cover. Then color the leprechaun picture.

    Name of story character who found the lucky four-leaf clover:

_____

THE PERFECT VACATION FOR _____

Title of Story _____ Author _____

<u>Directions</u>: Select a character from the story. Explain where that character would most like to take a vacation and tell why. Use your imagination and come up with an interesting vacation idea and a logical explanation of why the character would want to go there.

_____

_____

_____

_____

_____

_____

_____

_____

_____

_____

_____

_____

_____

_____

_____

_____

Continue writing on another page.

I'M YOUR FAIRY GODMOTHER!

Title of Story _____ Author _____

Select a character from the story. Imagine that you are that character's fairy Godmother and that you have strong magical powers. On another sheet of paper, write a story telling how you would make yourself known to that character and how you would use your powers to change or help that character. When you have finished, staple this page to your story to make a cover.

NAME _____

MEET YOUR SUBSTITUTE TEACHER

Title of Story _____ Author _____

Select a character from the story you just read. Imagine that character is your substitute teacher for the day. Write a story about your day at school with that new teacher.

Write your story on notebook paper. When you have finished, staple this page to your story to make a cover.

Name of the story character substitute teacher:

_____

PICTURE THAT PLACE!

Title of story _____ Author _____

Draw a picture of the place in which this story took place.

Write 5 different words that describe the place pictured above.

_____   _____

_____   _____

_____

NAME _____

SUDDENLY A MILLIONAIRE!

Title of Book _____ Author _____

Main Character _____

$$

Suppose the main character of this story was suddenly given one million dollars! How do you think he or she would have spent it? List the ways and explain why you think he or she would have spent the million dollars in that manner.

_____

_____

_____

_____

_____

$$

DESCRIBE THAT CHARACTER!

TITLE OF STORY _____ AUTHOR _____

Name of story character _____

Age _____   Male   Female   *(Circle one)*

Physical appearance

_____

_____

Personality

_____

_____

Behavior

_____

_____

Likes

_____

_____

Dislikes

_____

_____

FIRST . . . NEXT . . . NEXT . . . LAST

Think about the story you have read. In the first box below, draw a picture of what happened first in the story. In the second box, draw a picture of what happened next. In the third box, draw a picture of what happened next. And in the fourth box, draw a picture of what happened last.

Title of Story _____

Author _____

1.	2.
3.	4.

DEAR SIR

Title of Story _____ Author _____

Write a letter to the publisher of your reading book. Indicate your enjoyment of the story you just read and explain why you think the story should be included in the next edition of the reading book.

NAME _____

DEAR AUTHOR

Title of Story _____ Author _____

Write a letter to the author, telling him or her the part of the story you liked best. Continue your letter on the back of this page if you need more space to finish the letter.

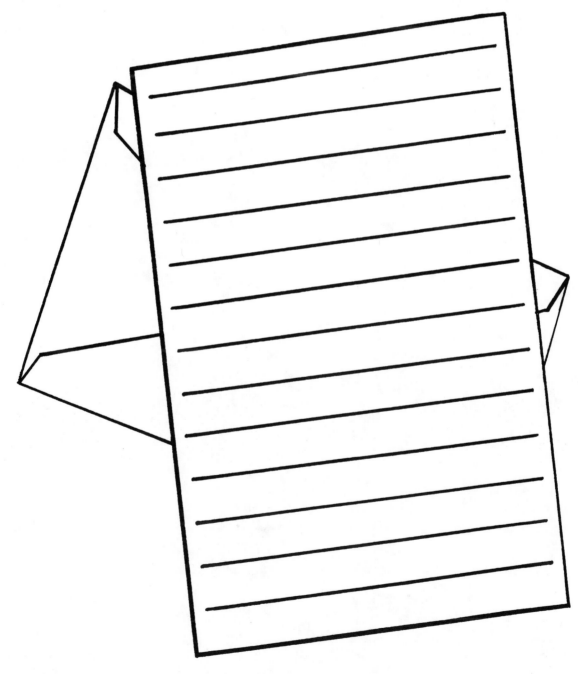

Section 14

BOOK REPORT FORMS TO MOTIVATE READING

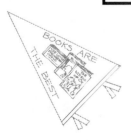

BIOGRAPHY
(GRADES 3-6)

Set up a display table of good biography books appropriate for your grade level. Your school librarian or the children's librarian at your local public library can assist you in finding good biography books for your display.

Ask students to select a biography to read either from the display of biography books in the classroom or from the library. (If the students are not familiar with biography books, take time to explain what they are and show them where they are located in the school library.) Hold up several biography books with which you are familiar and know are good. Talk enthusiastically about them. Absolutely "sell" the students on wanting to read biography books. Then distribute a copy of the "Biography" book report form to each student. After the students have finished reading a biography book, have them write a book report on this form.

OPTIONAL FOLLOW-UP ACTIVITY

Designate a FAMOUS PERSON FROM THE PAST DRESS-UP DAY. Ask each student to dress up as a character from the biography he or she has read. Have them prepare a name sign to hold indicating the person they are representing. Make arrangements for your class to visit one or more other classrooms so that your students can model their costumes and tell a little bit about the person they are representing and show the book they read about the person.

225

BIOGRAPHY

NAME _____

Title of book _____ Author _____

Person the book was about _____ When the person lived _____

Why was that person important enough to have a book written about him or her?
_____
_____

What impressed you most about the character?
_____
_____

A SUPER TERRIFIC BOOK AWARD
(GRADES 3-6)

Distribute copies of the book report form, "A Super Terrific Book Award." Explain to the students that each time they read a really terrific book, they should fill out one of these awards for the book and hand it in to you. Hang the completed book awards on the walls around the classroom, in the hallway, or in the school library. Place a stack of extra copies of the book awards on a bookcase or book display table where students can help themselves as they need additional awards.

Encourage students to read each other's awards and begin to read some of the books highly recommended by their classmates.

A SUPER TERRIFIC BOOK AWARD

THIS CERTIFICATE IS AWARDED TO THE BOOK

_____

TITLE OF BOOK

WRITTEN BY

_____

AUTHOR(S)

FOR BEING A SUPER TERRIFIC BOOK TO READ!

Signed by

_____

Student who read the book

Date _____

School _____

Grade _____

228

THE YUCKY BOOK AWARD
(Grades 3-6)

Occasionally, students will select a book that, once they begin to read, they discover they really don't like it. This book report form allows those students to report their dislike of the book.

Distribute copies of "The Yucky Book Award" book report form. Explain to the students that occasionally they may select a book that they decide they really don't like. Tell them they have two choices with a book like that. One is to put the book back and select another book to read. The other choice is to continue reading the book, figuring that the book will probably get better once they are further into the book.

Explain to the students that any time they read all the way through a book and decide that it was a really lousy book, they can choose to fill out a "Yucky Book Award" form for the book. In that way they can notify other students of their reaction to the book. Point out to the students that they will possibly never have to use this form, since most books they will select to read are really good books. But the form is there in case they need it. Place extra copies of "The Yucky Book Award" form on a bookcase where students can help themselves as needed.

Remember to tell students that just because someone doesn't like a particular book, it doesn't mean that someone else wouldn't like the book. Students should be open-minded.

THE YUCKY BOOK AWARD

Title of Book _____

Author of Book _____

Specific reasons why I didn't like this book and think it deserves THE YUCKY BOOK AWARD

_____

_____

_____

Signature _____

NO TRICK—THIS BOOK WAS A TREAT
(Grades 3-6)

Distribute a copy of "No Trick—This Book Was a Treat" to each student. After students have finished reading a good library book, have them write a brief book report on this motivational book report form. You may wish to suggest they write a rough draft of what they want to say about what happened in the story on another piece of paper. Then, after they have proofread and edited what they have written, they can copy the perfected version onto the book report form.

When they have finished filling in the information on the form, they can lightly color in the picture. The completed forms can be displayed so that students can look at each other's reports.

NO TRICK—THIS BOOK WAS A TREAT

Name of book _____ Author _____

Main Characters

_____

_____

What Happened in the Story

_____

_____

_____

_____

_____

_____

_____

_____

WANTED: AN OUTSTANDING BOOK FOR GOOD READING
(GRADES 3-6)

Distribute copies of the "Wanted: An Outstanding Book for Good Reading" book report form. Explain to the students that each time they read a really good book, they should fill out one of these posters on the book and hand it in to you. Hang the completed "Wanted" posters on the walls around the classroom. Place a stack of extra copies of the forms on a bookcase or book display table where students can help themselves as they need additional posters.

Encourage students to read each other's "Wanted" posters and begin to read some of the books highly recommended by their classmates.

WANTED

AN OUTSTANDING BOOK
FOR GOOD READING

(Draw a picture that in some way represents the book.)

Name of Book _____

Description of Book:

_____

_____

_____

_____

_____

Reason why this book is on this BOOK WANTED FOR GOOD READING poster:

_____

_____

_____

BOOK BUBBLES
(GRADES 3-6)

Distribute a copy of "Book Bubbles" to each student. After students have finished reading a library book, have them write a book report on this book report form. When students have finished filling in the book report forms, display the forms so that students can read each other's book reports.

NAME _____

BOOK BUBBLES

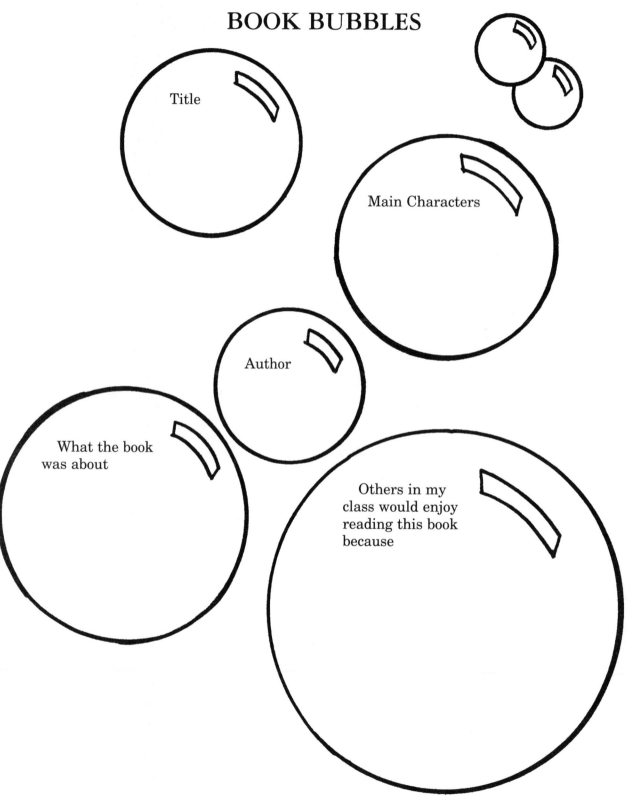

LEAFING THROUGH A GOOD BOOK
(GRADES 3-6)

Distribute a copy of "Leafing Through a Good Book" to each student. After students have finished reading a library book, have them write a book report on this motivational book report form. When they have filled in the information on each leaf, have them outline the leaf and lightly shade in the inside edges with crayons or colored pencils. The leaves can be colored green or in fall colors.

The completed book report forms can be displayed on the wall in the hallway for other students' viewing.

LEAFING THROUGH A GOOD BOOK

NAME _____

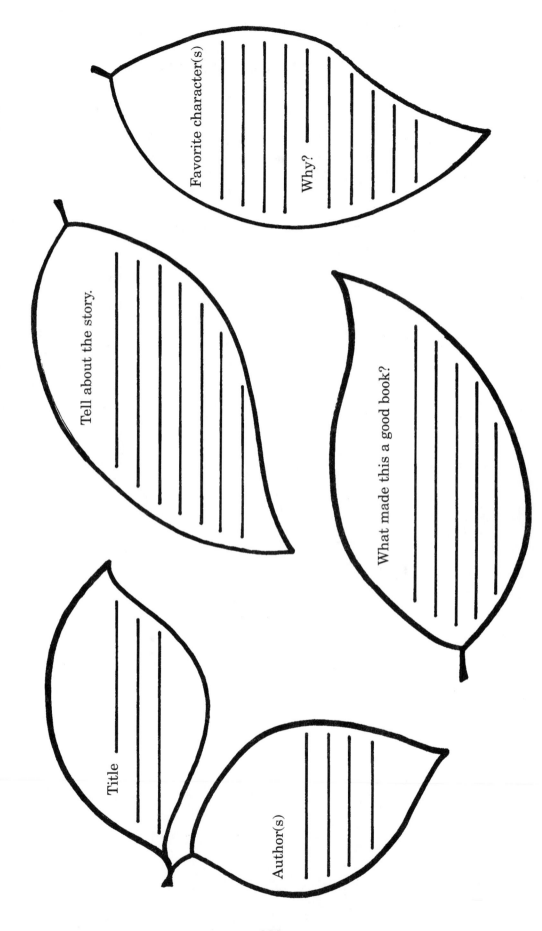

Favorite character(s)
_____
_____
_____
Why?
_____
_____
_____

Tell about the story.
_____
_____
_____
_____
_____
_____

What made this a good book?
_____
_____
_____
_____
_____

Title
_____
_____

Author(s)
_____
_____

SUPER BOOK POWER
(GRADES 4-6)

Distribute a copy of "Super Book Power" to each student. After students have finished reading a library book, have them write a book report on this motivational form. When they have finished filling in the information, they can use crayons, colored pencils, or markers to color the page to make it look as though colorful fireworks are exploding.

Display completed book report forms on a bulletin board for other students' viewing.

SUPER BOOK POWER

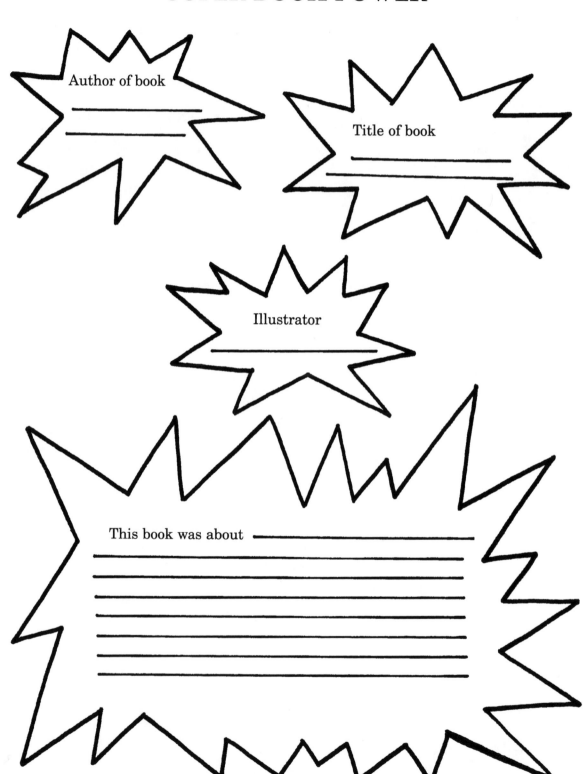

THE ENDING AFTER THE ENDING
(GRADES 4-6)

Talk about the fun of reading a good book. Tell the children that many times when you have reached the end of a great book, you wished the story could have gone on and on. Ask how many students have had this feeling about a book they have read.

Distribute a copy of "The Ending After the Ending" to each student. Call on a student to read aloud the explanation and directions at the top of the page. Ask the students to write an "ending after the ending" for the next good book they read.

VARIATION

You may wish to distribute copies of "The Ending After the Ending" to the students after you have finished reading aloud a book that the whole class has enjoyed. The students can then write individual "endings after the ending" for the story. These endings can be bound into a class book of new endings for the story. The students can then read and enjoy each other's new endings.

THE ENDING AFTER THE ENDING

How many times have you come to the end of a really good story and wished it would continue? The story was just so good you wished it would continue on and on!

Here is your chance to become the author and continue writing the story in the book you have just completed reading! Think of what might happen next and write it in the way the real author might have written it. Turn your imagination loose and have a good time!

Title of Book _____ Original Author _____

_____

_____

_____

_____

_____

_____

_____

_____

_____

_____

_____

_____

_____

_____

Continue on additional paper, if needed.

A GOOD BOOK FOR READING WHILE SHIPWRECKED ON A DESERTED ISLAND
(Grades 4-6)

Talk about what it would be like being shipwrecked on a deserted island for a long time. Talk about how a book could be a *real* treasure to help pass the time. Have some of the students suggest good books they have read in the past that they wouldn't mind having along if they were shipwrecked.

Distribute a copy of "A Good Book for Reading While Shipwrecked on a Deserted Island" to each student. Explain that after they have finished reading a really good book, they should write the book report on this form. Suggest that when they have finished filling in the information, they might wish to take a blue crayon or colored pencil and lightly color the water area on the page.

Hang the completed book report forms on a bulletin board or a wall for other students' viewing. In this way, students can get ideas from each other of books they might want to read next.

NAME _____

A GOOD BOOK FOR READING WHILE SHIPWRECKED ON A DESERTED ISLAND

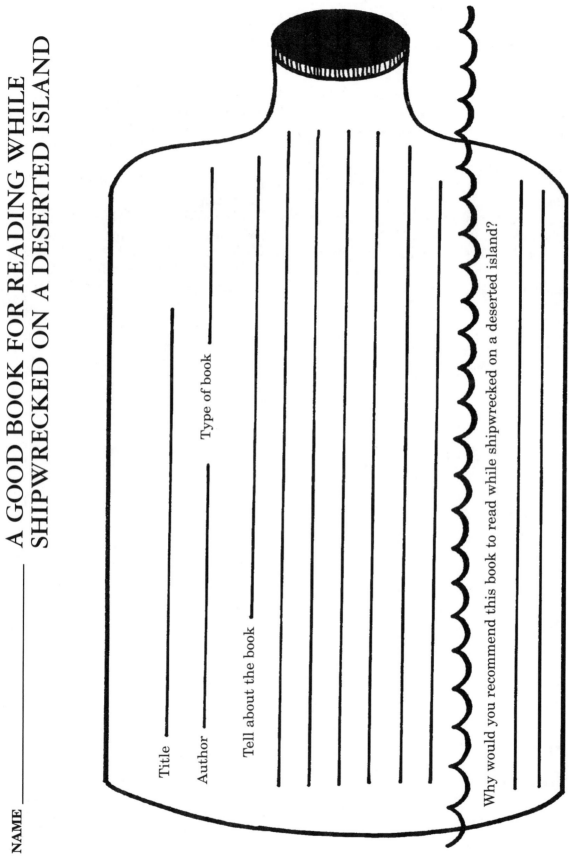

Title _____

Author _____

Tell about the book _____

Why would you recommend this book to read while shipwrecked on a deserted island? _____

© 1995 by Patricia Tyler Muncy

244

THE JUDGE'S SCORE CARD
(GRADES 5-6)

Distribute a copy of "The Judge's Score Card" to each student. Place an additional stack of forms in an easily accessible location where students can pick up additional copies as they read more books. Explain to the students that when they finish reading a library book, they are to fill out a score card on the book, rating various aspects of the book as outstanding, good, fair, or poor. Have students turn in the completed score cards. Punch holes in them with a hole punch and keep them in a looseleaf notebook. Tell the students where you will place the notebook and encourage them to occasionally leaf through the notebook to see which books are highly rated by their classmates.

Occasionally, you may want to look through the notebook, noticing books that are rated high by students. You can then, with notebook in hand, point those books out and really give a "sales pitch" on those books to your students. This will convey to students that it is worthwhile filling out a score card on the books they read. It will also lure a number of students into reading the books highly rated on the score cards.

THE JUDGE'S SCORE CARD

TITLE OF BOOK _____

AUTHOR _____

PUBLISHER _____ COPYRIGHT DATE _____

Judge the book only after careful reading. Rate the book in each of the following areas.

	OUTSTANDING	GOOD	FAIR	POOR
INTERESTING CHARACTERS	_____	_____	_____	_____
EXCITING STORY	_____	_____	_____	_____
GOOD ENDING	_____	_____	_____	_____
GOOD DESCRIPTIONS	_____	_____	_____	_____
A BOOK TO RECOMMEND TO OTHERS	_____	_____	_____	_____

COMMENTS _____
_____
_____

OVERALL RATING   _____   _____   _____   _____

SIGNED _____
NAME OF JUDGE

DATE _____
DATE JUDGING TOOK PLACE

ADVERTISE THAT BOOK!
(GRADES 5-6)

Explain to the students that when they have finished reading the book they are currently reading, you want them to create a picture poster to advertise the book. You may wish to bring in some magazines with full-page advertisements, have the students study those advertisements, and discuss some of the characteristics of good advertisements. You may also wish to borrow a couple of copies of a magazine called *Publishers Weekly* from your local public library. This magazine will have full-page advertisements of books. Students can also look at some of these advertisements.

Next, distribute copies of the "Advertise That Book!" book report form. Encourage the students to plan their advertisements carefully. Explain that they can use colored pencils, crayons, markers, and other media to create their advertisements.

Display completed advertisements in the school library or other high visibility location in the school.

ADVERTISE THAT BOOK!

Make a picture poster to advertise the book you have read. Make your poster so interesting that others will want to read the book! Be sure to include the title and author of the book on your poster.

Section 15

INDIVIDUAL
STUDENT
READING RECORD
PAGES TO
PROMOTE
READING FOR
PLEASURE

BARRELS OF GOOD BOOKS

Distribute a copy of "Barrels of Good Books" to each student. Have each student write his or her name at the top of the page.

Explain to the students that they are to fill in a barrel on their page each time they read a good book. Tell them that when all students in the class have finished filling in the barrels on their Reading-Record Page, you will take them to the local public library where the librarians will set up a display of their "Barrels of Good Books." Children—and adults coming to the public library to select books for children—will see the display and read the titles of the books that are recommended as being good. Explain that as they finish reading a good book, they must decide whether it was really good because, if they put it on a barrel on the Reading Record Page, they are in fact recommending it as a good book to children and parents all over the town or city.

Collect the "Barrels of Good Books" and put them in a file folder in an easily accessible location.

Explain to the students that, when they are ready to add a book to their Reading Record Page, they should find their page in the folder, fill in the needed information, and return the page to the folder. By keeping the Reading Record Pages in the folder, they will stay neat and clean.

When students have finished filling in the barrels, let them lightly color the barrels, being careful not to cover up and make unreadable the book information on the barrels. Then take the completed Reading Record Pages to the public library closest to you and have the librarians set up an attractive display.

Then, encourage the students to take their parents to the public library to see the display and to select some books to read while they are there.

NOTE

Prior to introducing this activity, it is essential that you contact your public library and make arrangements for the display. The library will probably gladly allow a week or two, perhaps even a month, for the display. However, they will want to schedule when the display will be appearing in the library. This means you will have to have in mind a feasible date by which the Reading Record Pages will be completed and ready to be taken to the public library.

BARRELS OF GOOD BOOKS

NAME _____

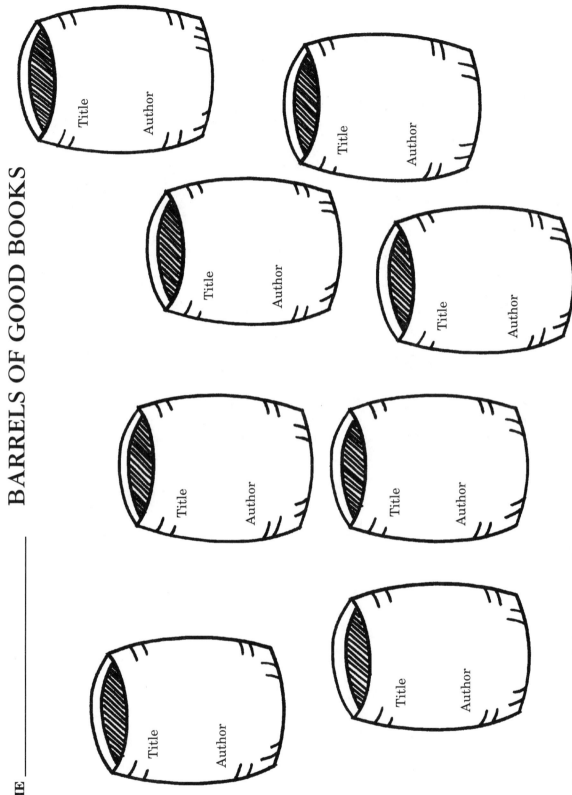

READING RECORD PAGE

HOT DOG! THESE WERE REALLY GOOD!

Distribute a copy of "Hot Dog! These Were Really Good!" to each student. Have each student write his or her name on the page.

Explain to the students that each time they read a terrific book—one about which they feel like shouting, "Hot Dog! This was a *great* book!" when they've finished reading it—they should get out this Reading Record Page and fill in the title and author of the book on one of the hot dog buns, then *lightly* color in that hot dog bun.

Distribute a file folder to each student. Ask each student to write his or her name on the file folder tab and insert the "Hot Dog! These Were Really Good!" page into the folder. Collect the file folders and place them in a file folder holder in an easily accessible location.

Tell the students that the object is to fill in all of the hot dog buns with the titles and authors of really good books. Explain that when they have finished filling in all of the buns on their Reading Record Page, they should give you the page so that you can hang it on the wall. Point out that they can then look at each other's pages on the wall for titles of really good books they may want to read.

NAME _____

HOT DOG! THESE WERE REALLY GOOD!

Whenever you finish reading a REALLY, REALLY good book, write the title and author of the book on a hot dog bun.

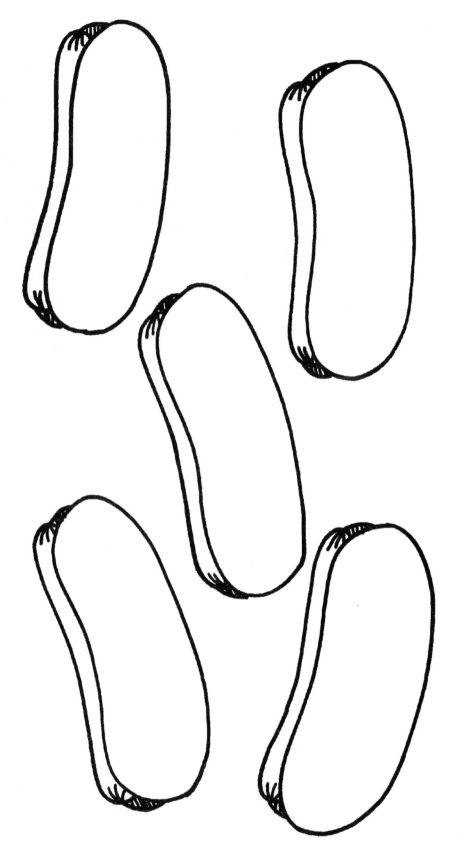

READING RECORD PAGE

KEEPING TRACK OF GOOD BOOKS!

Distribute a copy of "Keeping Track of Good Books" to each student. Have each student write his or name on the page. Then collect the Reading Record Pages and place them in a stack on a bookcase.

Explain to the students that each time they read a good book, they are to come to the bookcase, find their own Reading Record Page, fill in the title and author information on a footprint, then put the page back on the stack for safekeeping. Tell them that as soon as several students have completed filling in each of the footprints with the names of newly read, really good books, you will display their Reading Record Pages in the school library. Mention that as additional students complete their footprints, their Reading Record Pages will be added to the display.

Point out that other boys and girls in other classrooms in the school will be referring to their book recommendations on the displayed Reading Record Pages, so they should carefully decide, as they finish reading a book, whether it was good enough to deserve being put on their Reading Record Page and recommended to other students in the school.

After students have finished filling in all of the footprints on their Reading Record Pages, have them lightly color the footprints with crayons or colored pencils before displaying them in the school library.

KEEPING TRACK OF GOOD BOOKS!

NAME _____

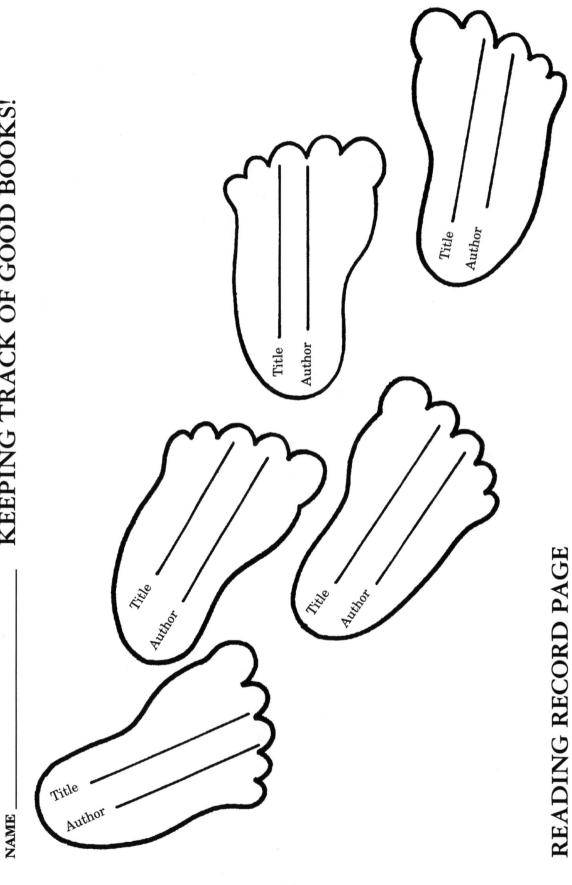

READING RECORD PAGE

I AWARD THESE BOOKS A RIBBON

Distribute a copy of "I Award These Books a Ribbon" to each student. Have each student write his or name on the page. Then have the students hang their pages neatly on a bulletin board or wall.

Place a container with blue, red, and yellow felt-tip markers or colored pencils near the display area. Tell the students that each time they read a really good book, they are to remove their page from the display area and fill in the book title and author on a ribbon. Then they should color the ribbon blue, red, or yellow, using the following key:

blue = a GREAT book
red = a really good book
yellow = a good book

Only the center circle area with the book title and author's name should be left uncolored so that others can easily read the book information on the ribbon. After filling in a ribbon, the page should be returned to the display. The students should follow the same procedure each time they read a book worthy of being designated as a blue, red, or yellow ribbon book until all three ribbons are filled in.

Point out to the students that they can look at each other's ribbons for titles of books they may want to read.

NAME _____

I AWARD THESE BOOKS A RIBBON

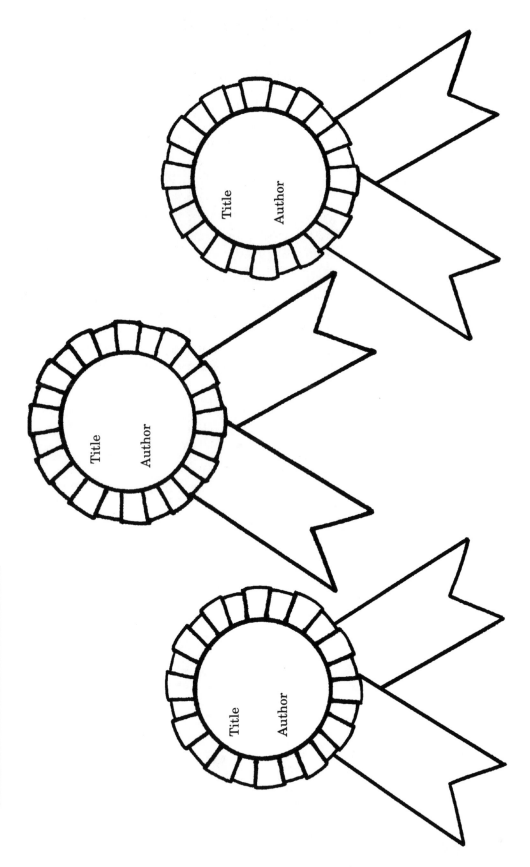

Title

Author

Title

Author

Title

Author

READING RECORD PAGE

258

BOOKS WORTH CROAKING ABOUT

Distribute a copy of "Books Worth Croaking About" to each student. Have each student write his or her name on the page and color the frog and the one lily pad that the frog is on with crayons, markers, or colored pencils. Distribute a file folder to each student. Ask the students to write their names on the file folder tab and insert the Reading Record Page into the file folder.

Explain to the students that they are to fill in a lily pad on the page each time they read a good book. Explain that the object is to fill all of the lily pads on their page as quickly as possible. Tell them that you want them to keep their Reading Record Page in the file folders you passed out and that you will keep their file folders in a holder for them. When they finish reading a good book, they should get their file folder, fill in the information, and return the file folder to its holder.

Collect the file folders and place them in a holder in an easily accessible location. When individual students have finished filling in all of the lily pads on the page, display those completed reading record forms on a wall or bulletin board.

BOOKS WORTH CROAKING ABOUT

NAME _____

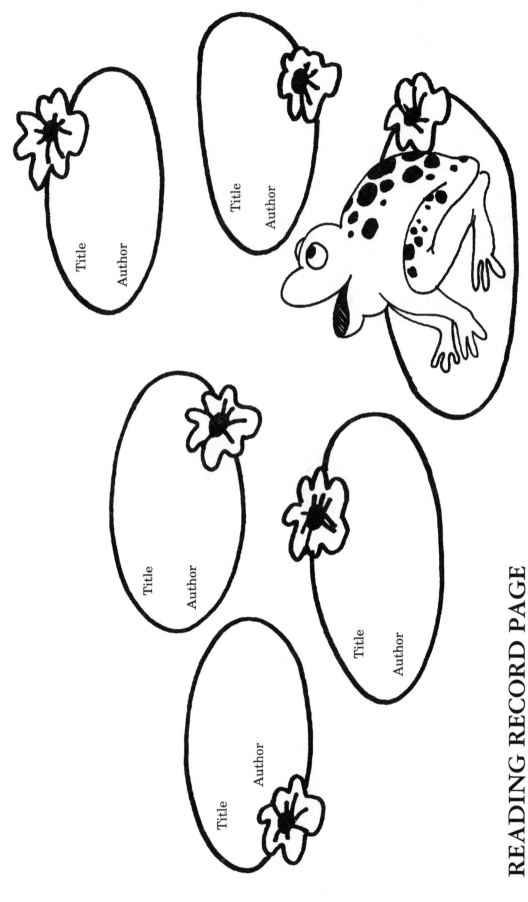

Title

Author

Title

Author

Title

Author

Title

Author

Title

Author

READING RECORD PAGE

SIGNS OF GOOD BOOKS

Distribute a copy of "Signs of Good Books" to each student. Have each student write his or her name on the page and color the grass green with crayons, markers, or colored pencils. Collect the papers and hang them on the wall.

Explain to the students that they are to fill in a sign on their page each time they read a good book. Explain that the object is to fill in all of the signs on their page as quickly as possible. Point out that they can look at each other's signs for titles of books they may want to read.

SIGNS OF GOOD BOOKS

NAME _____

READING RECORD PAGE

I GOT A BANG OUT OF THESE!

Distribute a copy of "I Got a Bang Out of These!" to each student. Have each student write his or her name on the page.

Explain to the students that you are going to collect the papers and hang them on the wall. Explain that each time they read a really good book, they should find their paper, take it down from the wall, fill in the title of the book and the author on one of the sticks of dynamite, lightly color the dynamite red with a crayon or colored pencil, and hang the page back up on the wall again. Tell them that the objective is to fill in the entire page with the names of good books they have read. Point out that they can look at each other's pages for titles of books they may want to read.

I GOT A BANG OUT OF THESE!

READING RECORD PAGE

DELICIOUSLY GOOD BOOKS

Distribute a copy of "Deliciously Good Books" to each student. Have each student write his or her name on the page, then lightly color the ice cream cones using colored pencils.

Explain to the students that they are to fill in an ice cream cone each time they read a "deliciously good book." Explain that the object is for each student to fill in all of the ice cream cones on their page.

Collect the Reading Record Pages from the students and place them in a bright colored notebook. On its cover you have printed DELICIOUSLY GOOD BOOKS and drawn ice cream cones. Explain to the students that each time they are ready to fill in an ice cream cone, they are to get the notebook, turn to their own Reading Record Page, fill in the book information, and then put the notebook back in its place for the next person's use.

Explain that when all of the Reading Record Pages in the notebook have been completed, the class will have a fantastic listing of "deliciously good" books. They will want to refer to this notebook often for ideas of great books recommended by their classmates.

DELICIOUSLY GOOD BOOKS

NAME

Title

Author

Title

Author

Title

Author

Title

Author

Title

Author

Title

Author

Title

Author

READING RECORD PAGE

READING RECORD PAGE CHARTS

The following twelve pages contain "Reading Record Page Charts" with seasonal themes. These charts are great for use in a literature-based reading program or in a whole language program, as well as a way to encourage children to read beyond the basal in a basal-reading program. They could become the base of students' reading portfolios. Or, students could contract with the teacher to read a certain number of books in a given time, in which case, these charts can be the recording device students will use to show books read.

Since most of the Reading Record Page Charts have seasonal illustrations, appropriate ones can be selected for the various times of the year. You may wish to distribute a different one each month, every six weeks, or every grading period. Twelve have been provided to allow you to pick and choose ones that best fit into the timeline you select or the interests of your students.

When you distribute copies of a Reading Record Page Chart to your students, be sure to have extra copies of the chart readily available for your students. When a student fills up a chart, he or she can get another copy and continue reading and recording books. The Reading Record Page Charts for the time period can then be stapled together. In this way, students will not feel limited to reading just nine books because there are just nine recording spaces on the Reading Record Page Chart.

You will quickly find that your students will enjoy filling in the Reading Record Page Charts, so put these charts to good use!

READING RECORD PAGE CHART

Yea, Books!

HORRAY for Books!

NAME _____

Date Completed	Title of Book	Author	Book Rating	Number of Pages

Book Rating Scale:

5	4	3	2	1
Fantastic	Very Good	Good	Fair	Boring

© 1995 by Patricia Tyler Muncy

268

READING RECORD PAGE CHART

NAME _____

Date Completed	Title of Book	Author	Book Rating	Number of Pages

Book Rating Scale:

5	4	3	2	1
Fantastic	Very Good	Good	Fair	Boring

READING RECORD PAGE CHART

NAME _____

Date Completed	Title of Book	Author	Book Rating	Number of Pages

Book Rating Scale:

5	4	3	2	1
Fantastic	Very Good	Good	Fair	Boring

© 1995 by Patricia Tyler Muncy

© 1995 by Patricia Tyler Muncy

READING RECORD PAGE CHART

NAME _____

Date Completed	Title of Book	Author	Book Rating	Number of Pages

Book Rating Scale:

5	4	3	2	1
Fantastic	Very Good	Good	Fair	Boring

271

Reading Record Page Chart

NAME _____

Date Completed	Title of Book	Author	Book Rating	Number of Pages

Book Rating Scale:

5	4	3	2	1
Fantastic	Very Good	Good	Fair	Boring

READING RECORD PAGE CHART

NAME _____

Date Completed	Title of Book	Author	Book Rating	Number of Pages

Book Rating Scale:

5	4	3	2	1
Fantastic	Very Good	Good	Fair	Boring

Reading Record Page Chart

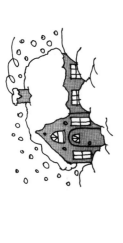

NAME _____

Date Completed	Title of Book	Author	Book Rating	Number of Pages

Book Rating Scale:

5	4	3	2	1
Fantastic	Very Good	Good	Fair	Boring

© 1995 by Patricia Tyler Muncy

READING RECORD PAGE CHART

NAME _____

Date Completed	Title of Book	Author	Book Rating	Number of Pages

Book Rating Scale:

5	4	3	2	1
Fantastic	Very Good	Good	Fair	Boring

READING RECORD PAGE CHART

NAME _____

Date Completed	Title of Book	Author	Book Rating	Number of Pages

Book Rating Scale:

5	4	3	2	1
Fantastic	Very Good	Good	Fair	Boring

© 1995 by Patricia Tyler Muncy

276

READING RECORD PAGE CHART

NAME _____

Date Completed	Title of Book	Author	Book Rating	Number of Pages

Book Rating Scale:

5	4	3	2	1
Fantastic	Very Good	Good	Fair	Boring

Reading Record Page Chart

NAME _____

Date Completed	Title of Book	Author	Book Rating	Number of Pages

Book Rating Scale:

5	4	3	2	1
Fantastic	Very Good	Good	Fair	Boring

READING RECORD PAGE CHART

NAME _____

Date Completed	Title of Book	Author	Book Rating	Number of Pages

Book Rating Scale:

5	4	3	2	1
Fantastic	Very Good	Good	Fair	Boring

Section 16

GUIDING PARENTS TO GET KIDS HOOKED ON BOOKS AT HOME

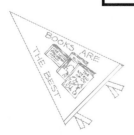

THE IMPORTANCE OF GUIDING PARENTS TO GET KIDS HOOKED ON BOOKS AT HOME

Parents who read to their children daily, who listen to their children read and talk about books, who promote reading as a leisure-time activity, and who provide their children with lots of books and magazines are the parents who are actively fostering their child's love of books and reading skill development. Oh, how we wish all parents would contribute to their children's learning in this way!

Since being read to daily and having lots of delightful books available to read and enjoy at home are so beneficial in fostering a child's love of books and reading, we must be sure we are providing all parents with information about the importance of a home environment that promotes books and reading. We must also give parents specific information on *how* to create a home that nurtures the enjoyment of books and reading.

We can provide parents with this information during parent-teacher conferences, during PTA/PTO meetings, and by sending informational newsletters or bulletins home periodically. The importance of your role in providing parents with this information cannot be over-emphasized. It is time, we as educators, stop complaining about a lack of a learning environment in the homes of many of our students and do something about it!

PARENT-TEACHER CONFERENCES—A PRIME OPPORTUNITY

Parent-teacher conferences provide a wonderful opportunity to guide parents in effective ways to create a home that fosters the enjoyment of books and reading. Almost all parents want their children to do well in school. And, since they see reading as the key to school success, they are most concerned about their children's reading skill development. They want their children to be good readers!

Many parents, especially the parents of children having difficulty learning to read, are literally begging for information on ways to help their children do better. Let's give them some concrete, effective ways they can help their children become better readers.

Here is a list of some suggestions you can incorporate into your parent-teacher conferences:

1. Discuss the importance of parents reading aloud to their children *every* day. If the parent is a single parent with a job and very limited time or the parent with minimal reading ability, you may want to inquire whether there is an older brother or sister, a baby sitter, a neighbor, or a grandparent who can read to the child each day.

2. Suggest that children have a bookcase in their bedroom that contains inviting books that entice children to read.

3. Recommend that parents include books as birthday and holiday presents.

4. Suggest to parents on tight budgets that children's books can be purchased very inexpensively at garage sales, auctions, used book stores, and Goodwill Stores.

5. Suggest to all parents that frequent trips to the local public library can be a source of wonderful books to place on the bookshelves and elsewhere around the house.

6. If you teach at a primary level, contact your local public library to find out about days and times of story hours appropriate for the age/grade level of your students. Then encourage parents to take their children to library story hours whenever possible. Provide parents with the information on days and times of the story hour.

7. Talk about the importance of parents setting a good example by letting their children see them reading and enjoying books and magazines.

8. Suggest that parents may want to set aside a half hour two or three nights a week when the TV is turned off and everyone in the family reads.

9. If you teach at the primary level, talk about the importance of parents listening to their children read aloud. Explain to the parents the importance of being patient and encouraging even if the child makes a number of mistakes while reading. Tell parents that when the child comes to a word he or she doesn't know, simply tell the child the word and let the child continue reading.

10. Explain to parents the importance of taking time to listen with interest when their children excitedly want to tell them about a good book they have read.

11. Talk to parents about the importance of promoting reading as a pleasurable leisure-time activity.

12. Provide parents with a list of some good children's books and magazines appropriate for children at your grade level. Include subscription information on the children's magazines.

After making the above suggestions to parents during the parent-teacher conferences, you may want to give them a copy of the "Promoting the Love of Books and Reading at Home" handout. The handout will provide parents with something to refer to (and refresh their memories) in the days, weeks, and months following the conferences.

PROMOTING THE LOVE
OF BOOKS AND READING AT HOME

Since reading is a skill that improves with practice, the more your child reads, the greater his or her reading skill development will be. Therefore, you want your child to enjoy books and reading and to read lots and lots of books. You are in a wonderful position to help your child develop that love of books and to foster reading, reading, and more reading.

The most effective ways you can help your child develop a love of books and reading are:

1. Read to your child every day. This is the single most important way you can help with your child's reading skill development and help your child develop a real enthusiasm about reading. Whether your child is in kindergarten or in the sixth grade, the time you spend reading good books to your child is time well spent!

2. Provide your child with lots of books. The more your child reads, the better he or she will read.

3. Find opportunities to give your child books as gifts.

4. Take your child to the local public library often. Your child will enjoy selecting books to read. In addition, the children's librarian will be very willing to help you select marvelous books to read aloud to your child.

5. Book stores, garage sales, auctions, and even Goodwill Stores can be sources of terrific children's books.

6. Children copy their parents in many ways. So, you will want to set a good example, letting your child see you reading and enjoying books and magazines. You would be surprised the influence this can have on your child.

7. Set aside a half hour or so two or three evenings a week when the TV is turned off and everyone in the family reads.

8. Make opportunities to listen to your child read aloud. If your child makes mistakes or doesn't know a word, be patient. Simply tell your child the word and let your child continue reading.

9. When your child has finished reading a really good book and just has to tell you about it, take time to listen to your child tell you about the story. Show sincere interest. You may want to ask some additional questions like: "What was the very best part of the story?" "Have you read any other books by this author?"